LIFE
IS NOT A
DRESS
SIZE

Other Books Available from Chilton

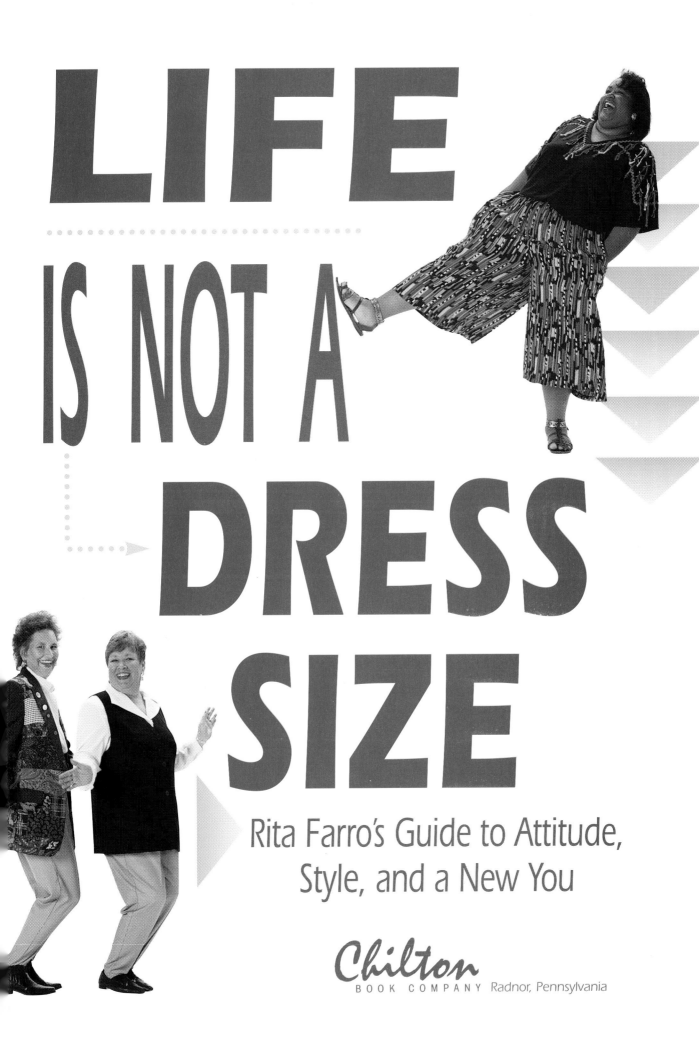

LIFE
IS NOT A
DRESS
SIZE

Rita Farro's Guide to Attitude,
Style, and a New You

Chilton
BOOK COMPANY Radnor, Pennsylvania

Designed by Anthony Jacobson

Photography by Debbie Willis, Boyd-Fitzgerald Studios

Illustrations by Rhonda Day, Boyd-Fitzgerald Studios

Manufactured in the United States of America

Library of Congress Cataloging-in-Publication Data

Farro, Rita.
    Life is not a dress size : Rita Farro's guide to attitude, style,
and a new you.
        p.   cm.
    Includes index.
    ISBN 0-8019-8758-X (pbk.)
    1. Fashion.   2. Clothing and dress.   3. Overweight women—Costume.
4. Beauty, Personal.   I. Title.
TT507.F33   1996
646'.34—dc20   96-20455
                                                               CIP

1 2 3 4 5 6 7 8 9 0   5 4 3 2 1 0 9 8 7 6

TO
JOHN

During
twenty-five
years of
marriage—
with many
ups and
downs—
you never
once made
my weight
an issue.

Contents

Acknowledgments

My childhood was a precarious balance of time spent wearing velvet Christmas dresses and digging in the dirt for fishing worms. Mom and Dad both showed me, every day, that the joy is in the work. The best thing they did for me was to give me four sisters and a brother: Ronda, Deborah, Deena, Wendy Ann, and Calvin. I think siblings are like broccoli. When you're a kid, you hate the stuff, but when you grow up, you develop a taste for it. Usually. I got lucky…

My husband's parents, Helen and John Farro, have long told me I should "write a book." They also loaned us the money to start our own business. No small risk.

When it comes to actually writing this book, Mary Mulari told me I should do it, and Nancy Harp taught me how to use my computer so that I could do it in this century. My sister Ronda provided daily support and encouragement. She was always there for me. Even when I wasn't in the state.

The Chilton Book Company gets the Publishing Medal of Honor. They went above and beyond the call of duty. Susan Clarey and Mary Green took a chance and signed me up. Robbie Fanning, with her ability to see the big picture, moved the book to another level. Marie Deer deleted my dashes and added just enough commas to prevent an epidemic of English teacher heart attacks. My editor, Susan Keller, skillfully and consistently made it a better book, without ever crushing my fragile ego. Tony Jacobson designed a book cover that popped and sizzled and his art layout mirrored my own personal style. Amazing. Sandy Cobb was an early fan and Bruce McKenzie was a late one. Nancy Ellis allowed the book to become her mission, as well as mine. Cathy Trefz took me to New York City and explained the business to me. This book was a team effort from the very start.

And the start was the moment Chris Kuppig "got it." I still remember the look on his face. At that very moment—in a conference room in suburban Philadelphia—this book began to breathe.

Hang on…I'm almost done. John, my husband, and my sons Ross and Elliott. I'm so proud of us. We bring out the best in each other—although it's taken a lot of practice, and it's almost never without some pain. I can't get too mushy, because they would really, really hate that. But I have to say one thing, boys: you are the wind, that's for sure.

Introduction

THE BIRTH OF A BOOK

Did you ever wonder how a book is born? This one came kicking and screaming out of my own life experience—and the realization that I was not alone.

I've been overweight most of my adult life. At some point, my size became a big issue for me. Not only was I unable to control my weight, but I had gotten to the point where my weight was controlling me. It was stopping me. I thought about it every single day, and I usually ended up feeling depressed. Then I would eat to make myself feel better, and before I knew it, I was wearing a size 22. Or rather, I would have been wearing a size 22, but I couldn't force myself to buy or sew anything that enormously big and ugly. So I literally had no clothes to wear; just leaving the house became a major trauma.

In 1986, my husband and I opened a fabric store. Sewing has always been a love of mine, but as I look back, I can't believe how this business decision changed my life. In order to go to work every day I had to have something decent to wear. So—as much as I hated the way my body looked—I was forced to make some clothes that actually fit me.

To say I was not enthusiastic is a bit of an understatement. Let's see…measure my awful, fat, overweight body. Sew something in a horrible size 22. Yeah, right. I would rather have stuck my wet tongue to a frozen pump handle. But I had to have something to wear to work, so I made some clothes that fit me.

Then it happened. Those clothes looked better on me than anything I'd worn in years. I was looking forward to getting dressed in the morning. I was feeling pretty good about myself. Every now and then, a customer would compliment me on my choice of pattern or fabric.

Introduction

I couldn't believe it: people were actually being nice to me! I was still fat, but my attitude was evolving. It was subtle at first, but I started to smile more. I wasn't so self-conscious all the time. Working with women who came into our store, helping them match just the right patterns and fabrics, was something I found I enjoyed—and being able to help them took me outside of myself and my own problems.

As I became more confident, I got more adventuresome with my clothes. My customers started commenting on my outfits even more, and telling me I looked great. I knew exactly what Mark Twain meant when he said, "I can live for two whole weeks on one sincere compliment." My personality started to show through my clothes, and people responded in a very positive way. They like me! They really like me! And this all happened in spite of my weight. That was a life-altering realization for me.

As the years went by, and I stumbled onto what styles and colors looked best on me, I got more and more comfortable with myself and my clothes. And the more daring I got with my wardrobe, the more fun I was having. In spite of my initial reluctance—even in spite of the fact that I still wanted to lose weight and be thinner!—I had developed a personal style.

Feeling more comfortable, looking good in my clothes, had changed my life forever, but still in my wildest dreams I could never have imagined what happened next. Mary Mulari, a nationally known sewing speaker, recommended me to Jolly Michel at Southwest Tech in Fennimore, Wisconsin. Jolly called and asked me to present a seminar at her sewing festival on designing clothes for the large-size woman. Jolly felt that I handled my "problem" with a unique style of dressing, and she thought other women my size would like to see my wardrobe.

Yikes! Public speaking?! I thought: these people must be crazy; I must be crazy to even consider it. Did you know that public speaking is one of the things we fear the most? It ranks right up there with death and snake bites. I was scared to death. They want me to get up in front of a roomful of women and actually talk about this? Being fat? Struggling to find styles I can wear? Trying to fit pants on my unfittable hips? How can I possibly talk about how a couple of double chins affects my choice of necklines? And besides: who would even come to my seminar? What would I call it?

Naming my seminar seemed like a huge problem. Should we call it "Fat Fashions"? Yeah, that'll pack them in. How about "Dressing the Overweight Body"? That didn't exactly have a ring to it. Besides, I had this gut feeling that nobody would even show up. Women who struggle with these issues surely don't want to walk into a room and hear another fat girl talking about "her" problems. Do they?

I decided to go for the chuckle. I've always been a big admirer of Cher, the epitome of a beautiful, successful, confident and sexy woman with an irreverent zest for life. I do feel like Cher most of the time. But the whole point here is that who I feel like and who I look like are two very different things! And people are always telling me that I remind them of Roseanne. That's a great compliment, too: Roseanne has an outrageous outlook on life and I've often felt like she was talking right to me. How can you not admire a woman whose philosophy of life is "Remember, girls: gravy is not meant to be a beverage!"?

So I called my seminar "How to Dress with Style When You Feel like Cher but Look like Roseanne."

I went on the road with my seminar, and I'll always remember the first big national show I was invited to. JoAnne Ross, the Director of the Sewing and Stitchery EXPO in Puyallup, Washington, called to tell me that my seminars were sold out. That really threw me. What does this mean? How can I do this? Am I in over my head? What was I thinking?

The night before I was to get on the plane for that first big trip, I was tucking my eight-year-old son into bed and he sensed that I was nervous and upset. Elliott asked me what was wrong, and I tried to explain it. I do believe you should always be honest and direct with children; but how could I tell him all about my stage fright and doubt? I just said, "Well, I have to get up in front of a room full of women and talk about how difficult it is to be fat in a country that worships thin people." He looked up at me and said, "Mom, don't worry. You'll be fine. You just tell those women out there that you know more about being fat than anybody in America."

So an expert was born. And every place I went, my presentations would sell out. Because that title said it all. Women got it right off the bat. I'm afraid those first seminars I did were awful—I simply packed up all the clean clothes in my closet, ate a few Hershey bars to build up my courage, and kicked into my one-woman style show with no beginning, middle, or end—but I knew I loved doing this. It was the biggest natural high I'd ever been on. Women were warm and enthusiastic, and my story seemed to touch a chord with them. "Cher/Roseanne" was a big hit.

I was still petrified every time I got up in front of an audience, but I was getting better all the time. After spending years being unhappy with my weight and letting it get in the way of my life, I was enjoying the challenge—no, thriving on the adventure and risk—of speaking all over the country. I remembered that years ago I had read somewhere:

You should do those things you are most afraid of.

I didn't get it then, but the day I walked onto that stage in Puyallup, Washington, with four hundred women in the room, and my heart in my throat, I understood. That day I decided I would always do the thing I was most afraid of.

So I accepted the invitations and became an experienced traveler: Florida, California, Las Vegas, Michigan, Wisconsin, Canada. Every major sewing show in the country invited me to come present "Cher/Roseanne," and I also began giving a "non-sewing" version of my seminar to general audiences and women's conventions. Women started asking for a book or some patterns they could use to develop their own personal style. I realized that if there was going to be a book like that, *I* would have to write it.

What a scary idea: me, write a book? What if it's awful? What if everybody hates it? Where would I even begin? Of course, since it was the thing I was most afraid of, I just had to do it.

And so, a book was born. ▪

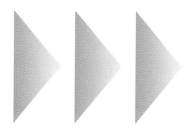

Part One

ADVICE TO THE GIFTED

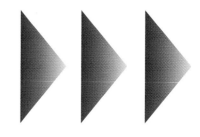

Chapter 1

THE MOMENTS OF YOUR LIFE

When I was sixteen, there was a song on the radio called *What's It All about, Alfie?* I used to listen to that song in my car and wonder about the line "Is it just for the moment we live?" Remember that line?

I'm not a kid anymore, but I still wonder about that line. Life is a funny thing. Nobody gets to play it back like a videotape. The moments happen when you least expect them. Once a moment has passed, you can never do it over or get it back. We have to learn to make the most of the moments, to cherish each and every one. Shared moments are the thread we use to weave our lives, the ribbons that tie real friends together. They are what makes a group of people a family.

I was raised on a farm in Iowa. There were six kids in our family: Calvin, Rita, Ronda, Debbie, Deena, and Wendy Ann. We were like a lot of families in the fifties. My dad was working two or three jobs and Mom stayed home with us kids. I have warm, fuzzy feelings about my childhood, though most of it is like a distant mist by now. I wish I had vivid memories of all the details, but most of that time has mushed together for me. I'm sure some people have sharp memories, but I've come to think my brain is pretty typical: after some years pass, the names, faces, and events settle down into the crevices of my brain like a warm fog.

Still, I do remember vivid moments. One day when I was nine, Dad and I were out in the apple orchard trying to get a kite up in the air. It was a beautiful, bright fall day, with a brisk, cool breeze. The sun was shining and big white clouds were moving through a blue, blue sky. I remember how special I felt. Maybe Dad only spent five or ten minutes with me and that kite, but I remember it as if it were yesterday. What a pretty, perfect day it was! Whenever I see a kid with a kite, I'm snapped back to that moment, and I can smell the apples. The kite almost took off, too!

The funny thing is that Dad doesn't have that same moment in his memory. He looked at me blankly recently when I asked him about this. It was not a typical thing for us to be doing. When I actually think about it, trying to fly a kite in an apple orchard doesn't make much sense. And how on earth did I get out of the house without Ronda or Debbie trailing me? Or Calvin stealing the kite? Maybe all those things are what made it a special moment for me.

My point is that you never know when you're going to have a moment. I don't think you can plan them, or orchestrate them, or control them in any way. You can't even know for sure that everybody in the room is having the same experience. But the moments are what make life worth living. So I guess Alfie was right: it is just for the moments that we live. They are the memories that enrich our lives and make us the people we are.

Our weight can stop us from having moments like that. Worse yet, that excess weight can be responsible for some very negative moments. I know this, because I've had depressing, negative moments because of my weight; you may have too.

Think class reunion. Now there's a potential moment! Twenty years after we graduated from North Scott High School in 1967, my best high school friend, Sue, was working on the reunion committee. They put together a wonderful event to reunite as many of the class of 1967 as possible. I really wanted to go: I bought the ticket; I had a new dress hanging in my closet; arrangements had been made for a baby-sitter. Then, at four in the afternoon, I had one of those moments. Only this was a bad one. They stick with you too.

At four in the afternoon, I sat on my couch, and it washed over me that I would probably be the fattest person in the room that night. Most of these people hadn't seen me in twenty years and I'd gained at least sixty pounds since then. How embarrassing would it be if they didn't even recognize me? Would they be shocked by my weight? Would somebody make a comment? Would they be whispering behind my back? All these doubts kept going through my mind as I sat on that couch.

At the last minute, I called Sue and made up an excuse not to go to the reunion. I just was not at a place where I could handle it.

I lost a moment that night. Nobody else missed anything, but I lost an opportunity to see and visit with people who had once been very important to me. I missed hearing about their families and telling them about mine. I shared a history with those people that I truly would have enjoyed reminiscing about. But it was a moment that only came around once. They all are. And I missed it.

Maybe you've missed some too. You are not alone. Thousands of women do the same thing. Trust me, I've talked to them in just about every state of the union! Having a weight problem is one thing; letting it determine how you live your life is quite another. We let the weight make negative choices for us. We become overwhelmed. We make it so important that we actually miss moments.

The best thing about the work I do now is that I get to meet other women who are struggling with the same issues I am, and hear their stories. After my "Cher/Roseanne" seminar at a big store in Wisconsin several years ago, a lady came over to talk to me. I'll call her Sally. Sally's story was that the factory she had worked at for seventeen years shut down when she was 53. She felt as though she'd never get a decent job again. When I met her, she'd been unemployed for three years and had gained over fifty pounds. She could not remember the last time she had bought herself any new clothes. With tears in her eyes, she told me that she had not been out of her house for almost three months.

I'll never forget how I felt when I heard this story; because when I looked at Sally, I saw an attractive woman! She was maybe a size 18 (don't I wish!), with a wonderful smile and great-looking thick dark hair. She was well-spoken and intelligent—yet she felt so worthless that she had made herself a prisoner in her own home.

Do you know why Sally came to my goofy seminar that day? Because the month before, her only grandchild had had a milestone and Sally missed it. The little girl was having her first real birthday party. You know the one: theme decorations, party hats, and little school friends. A pretty big moment for a six-year-old child—and her beautiful grandmother missed the party. Why? Because Sally couldn't bear the thought of all those people seeing that she'd gained that weight. And because she truly did not have anything to wear.

As she was telling me her story, I realized how much courage it took for her to get in her car and drive to my little show that day. I wanted to help Sally. I wanted to tell her she was entitled to some happiness. I wanted her to believe that she was a worthwhile person. My meeting with Sally stayed with me, and I kept thinking about the little girl in Wisconsin and wondering whether she missed her grandma the day of the party. Did she think Grandma didn't love her? Did she wonder why she didn't come? Would she have cared what size Grandma was?

Sally missed a precious moment in her granddaughter's life, and she would never be able to recapture it.

I kept thinking about how much Sally was missing. About how sad she was. About how much time she'd already lost. And that's when I decided I really would write this book. Not that I have all the answers! I don't even know what all the right questions are. But I do know that I used to be just like Sally and a thousand other women with similar stories. When they're telling me about their lives, their missed moments, I'm always thinking, "Been there. Done that." I missed that class reunion not because of my weight, but because of a problem in my own head.

Somehow, along the way, I did manage to change. I know that clothes are a pretty superficial thing. But they make a tremendous difference, not only in the way other people think about you, but also in the way you think about yourself. And no matter what size you are, you should be making an effort to wear something smashing that fits you right now. It will change everything. It did for me.

Please believe me. I want you to know that in 1992 I went to my twenty-fifth class reunion. I wore a great outfit with a big colorful bouquet of flowers sitting on my right shoulder. The skirt was a bright flowered affair, with an interesting, uneven, ragged hem. I had earrings that matched perfectly, a bold matching belt, and shoes that were out of this world. I felt terrific and had a wonderful time at that party.

What a difference five years can make. Why? Was I thinner in 1992? Not at all. The truth is, I had gained at least another twenty pounds since the reunion I missed because of my weight. The difference was in my own mind. It was all about how I felt about myself. I had discovered that I was the problem—not the weight, and certainly not other people. Me.

Please don't let your weight stop you from having a life—from reveling in and enjoying the moments you should be stringing together. After a seminar of mine in Atlanta, Georgia, a woman came over to me and was very complimentary about my presentation (a girl can never hear too much praise, you know!). She shared this thought with me. I don't know if it was original or if she was quoting somebody, but I wrote it down and carry it in my purse.

Yesterday is history and tomorrow is a mystery. All we have is today—and the reason it's called the present is because it is a gift from God.

Chapter 2

BEAUTY IS ONLY SKIN DEEP, BUT UGLY GOES CLEAR TO THE BONE

America is obsessed with weight and money. Think about the cliché "You can never be too rich or too thin."

Does anybody really believe that having money will ensure happiness? How much money is enough? I think having a lot of money can actually cause grief and sadness. If your name is Rockefeller or Kennedy, can you ever be sure that somebody is being nice because they genuinely like you? Wouldn't you always be wondering if they were more interested in your money? Christina Onassis was one of the richest women in the world when she died, and I don't think she had a happy day in her life.

It's the same with the weight. Whether you believe it or not, no amount of weight loss can make you happy. If it could, you would never see thin people with problems. Have you seen the interviews on television with anorexic women? They are extremely thin, and extremely unhappy. Will they be happy when they lose twenty pounds? Fifty? Maybe a hundred? How thin is thin enough?

We women are too hard on ourselves. Way too hard. Think about how generous and forgiving we are when it comes to other people, and how impossibly critical when it comes to judging ourselves. We focus on our "problem" areas. We hate our hips; we are disgusted by our cellulite; we look in the mirror and all we can see is the double chin.

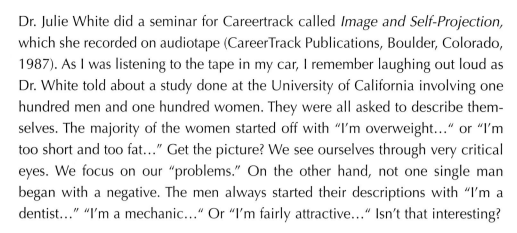

Dr. Julie White did a seminar for Careertrack called *Image and Self-Projection,* which she recorded on audiotape (CareerTrack Publications, Boulder, Colorado, 1987). As I was listening to the tape in my car, I remember laughing out loud as Dr. White told about a study done at the University of California involving one hundred men and one hundred women. They were all asked to describe themselves. The majority of the women started off with "I'm overweight..." or "I'm too short and too fat..." Get the picture? We see ourselves through very critical eyes. We focus on our "problems." On the other hand, not one single man began with a negative. The men always started their descriptions with "I'm a dentist..." "I'm a mechanic..." Or "I'm fairly attractive..." Isn't that interesting?

After the initial study, they went back and asked the men to describe a problem area. Do you know what the guys came up with? "I'm nearsighted." "I can't do the backstroke." Isn't that a hoot?

So what's going on here? I have to think that women are influenced by a gazillion-dollar beauty industry that is always telling us they can fix our *problems.* Men simply don't have to deal with this constant barrage of negative messages. Maybe that explains why they have such great self-esteem. (Notice I didn't call them self-absorbed.) The commercials for women are from Clairol telling us they can fix our hair. Or L'Oréal, or Vidal Sassoon, or Cover Girl, or Maybelline, or Jergens, or Massengill. Our hair is too gray or too straight; our hands are too rough; our teeth are too yellow; our lashes are too thin; our cheeks are too sallow. And then, of course, there's the entire weight of the diet industry bearing down on us!

Again, you have to wonder: is it the chicken or the egg? Did this beauty/diet industry build itself on the pillars of our insecurity, or did we get the insecurity from the industry in the first place?

Who can blame us? I've been "queen-sized" most of my adult life. Even these names are insulting. What does "queen-sized" mean? Are we named after beds? Would people call a small woman "twin-sized"? I don't think so.

Of course, maybe it's just awkward for people. Nobody wants to say *fat. Fat* is the biggest f-word in the English language. Heaven forbid anyone should use the word *fat.* But what do we want to be called? At this point in my life, I'd actually just as soon face the truth and call myself fat. So what? Some of the people I've loved the most in my life were fat, and it never mattered to me.

But in this day and age, I realize that people don't want to be called fat! Maybe you prefer that "queen-sized" thing. For crying out loud, I used to have to buy pantyhose at Kmart called "Big Mama"! We could go on finding new words for it forever. So here's the deal: I'm a size 22 (OK, OK: size 24). I'll call myself "average," and if you're bigger than I am, we'll call you "above-average," and if somebody is even bigger than you, we'll call her "gifted." How does that sound?

In fact, for the purposes of this book, I'll call all us big girls gifted.

Or course, this whole thing is more than a problem of semantics. Women have an extremely poor self-image. We are paranoid about being "fat." Taken to the extreme, this fear gives us anorexia. Young women are starving themselves and dying because they just can't get thin enough. In my mother's day, this was unheard of. Jane Russell, Marilyn Monroe, and Jayne Mansfield were the beauties of the forties and fifties: voluptuous, full-figured women. So what happened? What changed our national perception of beauty?

All I know is that in my life, it was Twiggy. It was June 1965; I was a sophomore in high school, and Twiggy invaded America via *Vogue* magazine. Actually, the Twiggy thing wasn't so much of an invasion as it was a bomb exploding in this country. Every girl I knew became unhappy with her body. I went right out and bought long, stupid-looking fake eyelashes, and I started taking diet pills. My size 13 body felt fat and unattractive to me. Could it be that anorexia is the very first illness created 100% by Madison Avenue?

Of course, I don't truly believe that some man in a gray pin-striped three-piece suit actually planned and orchestrated the Twiggy Invasion to demoralize and diminish the self-image of every woman in America, just so he could sell her more merchandise. Please don't tell me that happened. But from that time on, the average woman had to spend a fortune trying to look like Twiggy. Because it was an impossible dream, and she was supposed to be perfect, the spending never stopped. We all wanted to be like her. She was the beginning of a phenomenon that would eventually penetrate and pollute the very inner psyche of America. And the beauty industry certainly capitalized on the phenomenon.

What a marketing concept this must have been! The more unhappy women are with the way they look, the more money they'll spend. So there began a long line of unrealistically beautiful, excruciatingly thin, starving high-fashion models. From Twiggy to Kate Moss, thirty years of nonstop growth for the beauty industry.

In 1960, there was no real diet industry. According to Naomi Wolf in *The Beauty Myth,* by 1991 the diet industry had grown to an estimated $33 billion (New York: Wm. Morrow, 1991, page 17). Wow! Guess who the winner is in this scenario! Thirty years of empire-building on the backs of women who feel bad

about themselves. Thanks to the body image that started with the Twiggy phenomenon, we faithfully troop to weekly meetings, spending billions in our frustrating, nonstop search for somebody else's vision of perfection. The important thing to remember about the people collecting those weekly fees is this: they do not want you ever to be satisfied with your body, because then you would no longer need them!

Can you imagine your grandparents spending hard-earned money during the Depression to go to a weekly weight-loss meeting? Can you imagine them worrying about anything so ridiculous during the war years? My grandmothers would have been considered overweight by today's standards, but I can only imagine the look on my Grandma Dodds' face if somebody had suggested she spend fifteen dollars a week to get weighed-in in a church basement and an hour of her day discussing low-fat recipes!

We have been ill-used, girls. Our self-esteem has been under attack by a well-organized, expensive, high-speed, incessant advertising onslaught of mega-proportion. We have been made to feel ugly and unattractive just so people can make money off our misery—a misery largely *caused* by them in the first place! I don't think anything I can say will reverse the years of brainwashing. But maybe, just maybe, I can help you pull the hose out of your ear.

Here's a little quiz for you to take, to see how bad it is. Wait until you have a quiet ten minutes, and then sit down and answer these questions. Remember, there is no right or wrong answer here. Be honest!

S E L F - I M A G E   Q U I Z

Circle the response that best completes the following statements:

1. I think about my weight:
>   a. every day.
>   b. once a week.
>   c. once a month.
>   d. almost never.

2. I've been on a diet:
>   a. at least 100 times.
>   b. maybe 50 times.
>   c. just a few times.
>   d. never.

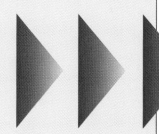

3. Most of the clothes hanging in my closet:

      a. fit me now.

      b. fit me two years ago.

      c. I can't remember when I last wore them!!

4. Fill in the blanks of this sentence:

      "If only I could lose _____ pounds, I'd go out and _____."

Answer True or False:

5. I have dreamed and fantasized about being a perfect size 10.

    True   False

6. I believe that if I lost weight, my life would improve.

    True   False

7. I'd give up 10 intelligence points to lose 25 pounds.

    True   False

8. I think my husband (or significant other) would be happier if I lost weight.

    True   False

9. I've made up an excuse not to attend an event because I was unhappy about my weight or my clothes.

    True   False

10. I believe that my weight has cost me a promotion or job offer.

    True   False

11. I think other people talk about my weight.

    True   False

Score your test:

1. a. 20 points	**2.** a. 20 points	**3.** a. 0 points
b. 15 points	b. 15 points	b. 15 points
c. 10 points	c. 10 points	c. 20 points
d. 0 points	d. 0 points	

4. If you thought of something immediately: 20 Big Ones!

If it took you more than five minutes to think of an answer: 10 points.

If you left it blank: 0 points..

5–11. For every True answer: 20 points.

    For every False answer: 0 points.

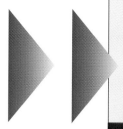

➠ If you scored over 200 points altogether, I recommend therapy.

➠ If you scored over 100 points, you're being too hard on yourself.

➠ If you scored less than 50, you're probably a handsome guy, and I can't imagine why you're reading this book!!

This quiz was a real eye-opener for me. I handed it out during every presentation of my Cher/Roseanne seminar, and soon I had over a thousand quizzes to analyze. Although the exercise was anonymous, there was a question at the bottom of the page that asked for the person's age, size, and weight. Here's the amazing thing: Even women I would consider a perfectly normal size thought about their weight every day. And these women believed life would improve if they lost weight. I was also shocked by how many young women were willing to give up 10 intelligence points if only they could lose weight.

Every last woman I surveyed was being way too hard on herself. How about you? What was your score? What can you do about it? It's easy for me to say "Lighten up!" But can you do it?

Here's the tough stuff.

Your weight does not determine your happiness.

Believe me? If not, go sit and watch the people in the psychiatric ward of a hospital sometime. Guess what? Just as many thin people as fat people. Maybe more! Isn't that amazing?

The problem is that we let the weight become an issue. We let it get in our way. We assume people will not take us seriously because we are overweight. We assume men will not be interested because we're too fat. We feel embarrassed to speak up in any public forum, because we don't want people to look at us and see our extra pounds. We do it. We are altogether too hard on ourselves.

Listen, I'd love to lose weight. My dream is to lose a hundred pounds and turn the title of my seminar around: "How to Dress with Style when You Feel like Roseanne but Look like Cher." But what if that never happens? Should I put my life on hold until I'm perfect? How long will that be? What will I miss in the meantime?

I'm not going to tell you that I'm happy with my weight. But I do want you to know that I am happy. Isn't that amazing? It wasn't always that way for me; I already told you that I felt so bad about my weight and the way I looked that I missed my twentieth high-school reunion. I was letting the weight control my life, and I was making wrong choices because of it.

I let the weight limit me. By the time I realized it, my life had become narrow and small. I was focused totally on myself, my weight problem, all the reasons I couldn't do things like buy new clothes or speak up at a public meeting. What kind of a life was that?

So how did I get from that place to this place? How did I get my life back? Is there one answer here, some magic, maybe a silver bullet?

No. I wish it were that simple. The truth is, it has been a journey. Not always smooth sailing, either. This trip had lots of twists and turns. Some false starts. Some wrong directions. But I've been learning every step of the way. Figuring this all out is like putting together a huge jigsaw puzzle. And each lesson I learned gave me one more piece of the puzzle. And the most amazing thing I learned is that my weight does not determine my happiness!

This is life-altering knowledge. I want you to believe it. I am not going to show you *the* pattern that will make you lose fifty pounds. Or *the perfect color* that will slenderize your body. But I can show you that great change is possible, even if you never lose a pound. My life has changed in a very positive and wonderful way. I've met hundreds of other women who tell me the same thing has happened to them. Once you take control of your clothes and establish a personal style, good things start to happen.

I'm not talking about spending a ton of money on the latest trendy clothes. Mostly, I try to ignore the fashion industry completely. This is about style. Not fashion. Let me show you how I see the difference between them.

Fashion versus Style

	FASHION	STYLE
CLOTHES	neon pink hot pants	a wool Chanel suit
SUPERHEROES	He-Man	Superman
CARPETS	avocado-green shag	Persian rug
MOVIES	*Lethal Weapon*	*Gone with the Wind*
FAMOUS WOMEN	Madonna	Jackie Kennedy Onassis

Get it? The important thing is developing your own style, not being a slave to fashion.

Your clothes not only send a clear message to the world, they also serve as a barometer for yourself, letting you know how you feel about yourself. I truly believe that. They are a reflection of your own self-esteem.

Happiness comes from inside. That's important for you to know. No matter what size you wear, you deserve to be happy. And you can be. Your weight does not determine your happiness. But your attitude does.

Your attitude. Not other people's. Remember, happiness comes from inside. Other people might have a problem with your weight. So what? You can't change them. You can only change yourself. That's the power every individual has. You can never change other people's negative attitudes. You can only change yourself.

> **Your weight does not determine your happiness.** ▪

Chapter 3

YOUR THREE SECONDS ARE UP: THE CRUCIAL FIRST IMPRESSION

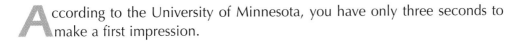

According to the University of Minnesota, you have only three seconds to make a first impression.

Three seconds—that's it? They must be kidding! What can anybody possibly notice in that brief period of time? Will they see that I'm a good person? Can they know that I'm a wonderful friend? How can they decide whether or not I'm reliable or honest? Geez.

When I finally grasped this concept, a lightbulb went off in my head. Suddenly it was clear to me why, when I saw a woman with pink sponge rollers in her hair, that's all I could remember about her (you must admit those rollers make a lasting impression). What about the times I ran into the local convenience store with no bra on? Who might have seen me then? They probably got a three-second gander. Does that mean I'll forever be a white-trash braless bimbo in their book?

Of course we all judge people. We do it every day, every place we go, to every person we meet. Usually, we don't even think about it; we just do it. But three seconds?! I had certainly hoped I had more time than that. I at least wanted to open my mouth and maybe tell a joke….

But I don't have more time. None of us do. The bad news is you have only three seconds to make a good first impression, and everybody in the world is judging you. They all notice what you look like and what you are wearing. Bummer. You know you can't lose any weight in those three seconds!

The good news is once you realize how important your clothes and your looks are, once you realize that people are judging you, you have a jump on things. Now you *know* that how you look and what you're wearing will be among the first things they notice! That's the deal. Because in three seconds, only the most superficial things will be considered.

So what can you do? And what do people really see in that first look?

According to Susan Fiske, psychology professor at the University of Massachusetts, the first three things people notice about you—things you have no control over—are assessed in a brief nanosecond. They are:

1. skin color
2. gender
3. age (in relation to themselves)

Think about it. If the Queen Mother walks into a room, you say to yourself, "There's a white woman who's older than I am." (She's older than everybody *I* know.)

Isn't that interesting? Remember: this just means that these things get noticed, not necessarily that they have a positive or negative impact on the person meeting you. They just happen to be the first things people see.

So what is the very important Number 4? What is the first thing people notice that you can actually control? It is your carriage. That's right, the way you carry yourself into a room: your posture, your smile, your eye contact.

Think about the impression you make if you slouch into a room, looking down at the floor and avoiding eye contact with everybody.

See this woman? She shuffles into the room, looking down at the floor. Her shoulders are rounded, and she can hardly wait to find a seat near the wall where nobody will notice her.

Now imagine yourself, the same day, the same room, the same you, the same clothes, but this time you thought about your carriage before you entered the room. You stride in with your head held high, your chin up, and a smile on your face. The people in the room are smiling back at you, aren't they.

Now look at this same woman again. This time, she's decided to stride into the room. Her head is up, she's comfortable, she's making eye contact, she's smiling, and people are smiling back at her.

What a difference!

The same woman, even the same clothes—but a very different first impression. This is a powerful message, and worth remembering. The cold, hard truth is that you never get a second chance to make a first impression. So how can you best control the impression you'll be making on people when you meet them?

That's what this book is about: taking charge of your own message. Developing a comfortable personal style.

No matter how much you weigh, you can still make a good first impression. Isn't that great? I don't know how I figured this out. Like many things in life, it was more of a process than a revelation. But however it happened, I have now fully evolved to the point where I feel comfortable and happy meeting a roomful of strangers.

Believe me when I tell you I make a great first impression—in spite of my weight! I control the messages my looks send to people, and within three seconds they know that I have a vigor for life and a great sense of humor, that I don't take things too seriously. They see a woman with a unique personal style. And they sense joy.

Let's face the truth. In three seconds, nobody can assess the really important stuff. They cannot know what our values are. They can't figure out whether we are trustworthy, reliable, or hardworking. The things I consider to be most important cannot possibly be evident in three seconds. But all the same, everybody is going to be influenced by that first impression, so it's important that we deal with it in order to positively affect the way other people feel about us.

If your clothes are tacky, ill-fitting, worn-out, boring or, worst of all, dirty: you just blew it. You will be dismissed. It's like wearing a sign on your back that says "Beat me. Ignore me. I'm worthless and I know it."

Chapter 3

If we do not value ourselves, how can we expect other people to value us? The impression we make on other people is the first step. We telegraph messages to people we meet. That's what our clothes do. They signal to the world how we feel about ourselves. Think about that for a minute. The way we look, the first impression we make…it's not only about what other people think of us, it's about how we feel about ourselves. It's about self-respect. It's about self-esteem. It's about getting past the weight and believing that our worth cannot be measured by a bathroom scale.

In order to make a difference in this life—to be heard and to have influence—you first have to deal with this crucial first impression. That is easier said than done. You have to believe that you are just as bright as anybody else in the world—and just as worthy.

You have to be good to yourself. You must believe that you are worth the effort. Buy some clothes for the size that you are right now. Spend as much money and time on your appearance as if you were a perfect size 10. Expect people to pay attention to you and listen to you!

Believe that you are an important and worthwhile person, and please, let this be reflected in the way you present yourself to the world. That's what style is all about. ▪

Chapter 4

DON'T BE YOUR OWN WORST ENEMY

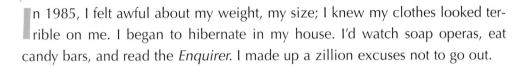

In 1985, I felt awful about my weight, my size; I knew my clothes looked terrible on me. I began to hibernate in my house. I'd watch soap operas, eat candy bars, and read the *Enquirer*. I made up a zillion excuses not to go out.

It would take me two hours to get dressed just to go to a Tupperware party at my sister's house. Remarkable, considering I only had one outfit. The pants were pull-ons, double-knit polyester, navy blue and white herringbone (yuck!); the top was a shapeless polyester number, and my shoes were thongs of the 99-cent variety. The inseams on the pants were completely worn through. I still shudder when I describe those clothes to you. I wore that hideous outfit for a year. That was my uniform. I had sunk to such a low point, that one outfit was all I had. I knew how awful I looked. I can still remember how worthless I felt when I put on those clothes.

The point is, nobody made me wear that outfit. It was a decision I made. I was punishing myself. I had become my own worst enemy, and I hated my body so much that I refused to spend money on clothes.

My attitude about the weight affected everything. I knew I looked awful, so I wouldn't buy anything new. Then, because I had no clothes that fit, I made up excuses not to go out. Then, because I felt sad that I wasn't going anyplace, I sat around the house and ate Cheetos to make myself feel better. So, of course, I gained more weight, and had fewer clothes that fit. It's a powerful negative snowball, believe me.

If, over the years, you have become your own worst enemy, chances are you've been feeling pretty low. Maybe you've neglected more than your personal appearance. Maybe you've lost touch with old friends, avoided family gatherings, made excuses not to be your child's room mother. Sound familiar? I hear these stories from women all over the country. We let the weight define us. We let it narrow our lives.

I met Pat in Denver. She was about five foot four, two hundred pounds, wearing a pair of pull-on double-knit black polyester pants with a cheap printed poly top (in a big, awful, floral print), old worn navy blue shoes, no makeup, and a shag haircut not of this decade. What was this girl doing with her first three seconds?

After my seminar, Pat asked me to go for a cup of coffee. She turned out to be a bright, educated woman. She had met her husband in high school and then worked as a waitress to pay for his college. He became a successful businessman while she stayed at home to raise four children, gaining weight with each pregnancy. Eventually, he ran off with his secretary. She was forced to go on welfare, and live in public housing. When she went back to college and got her teaching degree, she had to do her shopping (with food stamps) in the middle of the night.

The day I met Pat, she had been substitute teaching for six years and was unable to get a full-time job. Nobody would hire her, and as we were drinking our coffee, she started to cry. She described her last failed job interview (there had been dozens, but never a single job offer), and she was convinced that the reason she couldn't get hired was because she was fat.

Sure, that's a possibility. You and I both know there is a very definite fat prejudice in America. They did a whole show about it on *20-20,* and then Diane Sawyer did another one on *Prime Time.* (You can certainly trust today's investigative reporters to ferret out the big stories!) They seemed amazed that fat women didn't have the same opportunities as skinny women. Surprise, surprise! So we're not the fluff America wants in the front office. Our imperfect bodies don't fit in with their perfect corporate image. Maybe Pat is encountering fat prejudice. We all do, every day, in places we can't even imagine.

But as I visited with Pat that day, I kept thinking that she was her own worst enemy. Nothing anybody did could hurt her as much as she was hurting herself. And she can't change them. She can only change herself.

So I asked her a few questions:

- ❖ Why do you want to be a teacher?
- ❖ Are you a good one?

❖ Tell me why they should hire you instead of somebody else?

❖ What do you have to offer?

Pat's face lit up when she started to talk about teaching. Although she had been subbing for years, at all grade levels, her favorite age group was elementary. She felt like she could have a real impact on children that age. She talked about getting them motivated, discovering what special interests they had, helping to build their self-esteem, making a difference in their lives. I ask you, what more could a school want from a teacher?

So I asked her a few more questions:

❖ What did you wear to the job interview?

❖ Did you do your makeup?

❖ Did you have a new hairdo?

❖ Did you act comfortable and confident?

❖ Did you make a good first impression?

❖ Did you have references in hand from some of the principals you've taught for?

❖ Did you convey your enthusiasm to the administrators?

❖ Did you smile, Pat?!

When she started to think about these simple questions, she realized that the answer to every single one was no! Big surprise. Pat was being her own worst enemy. On her last job interview she had worn those same deadly polyester double-knit pull-on black pants, a red top, well-worn shoes, a scuffed, too-full plastic purse, no makeup, and that shapeless seventies hairdo.

HELL-OH, Pat?! This is your wake-up call! Whose fault is this? Did those school administrators decide that Pat was worthless, or did Pat decide that before she ever walked into the room?

Think about "worthless" for a minute. It means we feel worth...less. Less than anybody else. Less than the average woman. Certainly less than the skinny woman. We feel like we are without value. We put all that on ourselves, but why—because of some extra weight? Isn't this ridiculous! Why are we so negative? Why are we so hard on ourselves? What can we do?

That's the whole point, isn't it? We must learn to look in the mirror and see ourselves with kindness, not disgust. We have to consider our real worth.

Pat is a great teacher. She would be an asset to any school district that hired her. After talking with her for half an hour, I believed that. But could she? Could she see herself as capable and valuable? Could she convey that to a group of administrators in a position to give her a job? I feel like a broken record, but Pat's weight was not the problem. Her own attitude about it was the thing causing her great pain. She was wearing clothes that most women wouldn't be caught dead in. She had developed into her own worst enemy.

How about you? Here's a little quiz. Do you punish yourself? You might be surprised.

ARE YOU YOUR OWN WORST ENEMY?

Answer Yes or No:

1. Do you have clothes hanging in your closet that you haven't worn for two years?

   Yes   No

2. Have you ever worn the same pair of slacks three times a week because they're the only ones that fit you?

   Yes   No

3. Do you refuse to buy clothes "one size larger"?

   Yes   No

4. Because you won't buy clothes right now, has your wardrobe shrunk to fewer than four outfits?

   Yes   No

5. Have you ever stayed home from an event or a party because you truly had nothing that fit?

   Yes   No

6. Have you ever gone out in public in a pair of slacks that had the inseam completely worn through?

   Yes   No

7. If you must go clothes shopping, do you often leave the dressing room in disgust without buying anything because everything looks awful on your body?

   Yes   No

8. If you absolutely must buy something that day, do you make sure it's the cheapest possible thing?

   Yes   No

9. Have you ever bought something that was too small, telling yourself that it would motivate you to lose weight?

>   Yes   No

Check your answers. If you circled yes five times or more, watch out! Quit worrying about the fat prejudice in America. You have seen your enemy, and your enemy is within.

But what do you do then? I present a career workshop on dressing professionally and projecting a positive image to get ahead in the workplace. The day I met Pat, I knew she needed a mini-workshop. First: she had to change her attitude. She had to start believing that she would be an asset to any school that hired her. They are looking for good teachers…and she is one! Second: she absolutely had to repair the very poor, negative first impression she had been making. Remember the three-second rule.

Because Pat was desperate, and we didn't have a lot of time, I laid out some general rules to remember for job interviews.

1. Have an interview suit. That's right. Classic blazer is good. Skirt at knee length. A lovely blouse. Matching, polished, comfortable shoes. Make sure your purse is of good quality and neat in appearance. Every detail is important!

2. Have your hair done that day, if possible. Your makeup should be fresh, but not overdone. Wear little or no perfume.

3. Do your homework. Know about the school district. Prepare your credentials and resume to suit their needs. Have several letters of reference from principals you've worked for.

4. Be enthusiastic, Pat! We all know it's a big mistake to appear desperate on a job interview, but every employer I know would pay extra for a little enthusiasm!

5. Believe you are going to get this job, and SMILE. PLEASE SMILE.

Remember, you have only three seconds to make that first impression. It is true that for some people, in some situations, our weight is going to be an issue. So what? If that's the only thing they see or care about, it's their loss, not ours.

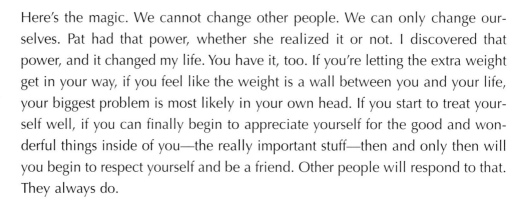

Here's the magic. We cannot change other people. We can only change ourselves. Pat had that power, whether she realized it or not. I discovered that power, and it changed my life. You have it, too. If you're letting the extra weight get in your way, if you feel like the weight is a wall between you and your life, your biggest problem is most likely in your own head. If you start to treat yourself well, if you can finally begin to appreciate yourself for the good and wonderful things inside of you—the really important stuff—then and only then will you begin to respect yourself and be a friend. Other people will respond to that. They always do.

Kathleen McKinney manages Added Dimensions, an upscale shop that specializes in plus sizes. Kathleen is often struck by how loving and supportive husbands of gifted ladies can be. Even when the women are beating themselves up, saying "No, I can't spend that much money—I need to lose weight first," the husbands are often telling them they look beautiful and deserve a new outfit! Do you believe it? Are we ready to believe that a man can love a woman who doesn't look like Cindy Crawford?

Gee, I have to hope so. In the same way money doesn't have anything to do with happiness, weight doesn't have anything to do with love. I've been married to the same man for over twenty-five years, and there have been many ups and downs. Some of our best times have been in the last two years, after I reached my top weight! The happier I am with myself, the happier we can be together.

So how do we get to that point? Let me tell you a story. The most important job I've ever done is raising my two boys. Years ago, after a particularly bad day at elementary school, Ross would go to bed sad and unhappy. I'd say, "Come on, smile for me." He'd refuse (of course). "I'm not leaving this room until you smile." Then, just to make me go away, he'd force a big goofy grin. And we'd both start to giggle.

I know it's too simple to sound important. But that's the magic of a smile. You can't *do* it and not *feel* it. Think about it. Is there anything more contagious than a smile? Try this little experiment. When you leave the house today, consciously decide to smile and make eye contact with the first three people you meet. I don't care if it's at the grocery store, in the street, or at the bank teller. Make eye contact and smile at them. See what happens. There is no better attitude adjustment in the world than just deciding to smile.

Believe me, I know this isn't easy. In the beginning, you will not want to do this. You won't want to smile, and you won't want to spend money on clothes. But I'm telling you this attitude adjustment is a major part of your growth as a person. (Okay, so maybe that's a poor choice of words. The last thing any of us needs is more growth....)

▶ Again—buy (or make) something for the size you are right now!

This is so important. It is absolutely revolutionary. This is the first step you must take to tell the world you're okay. That you believe you are a person of value. You'll be amazed at how good it feels to have clothes that aren't old or too worn or too ill-fitting.

Force yourself to wear clothes that fit well. Make yourself choose accessories that are bright and attractive. Spend a little money and time on your wardrobe. Talk yourself into applying for that promotion or speaking up at the next PTA meeting. You are an important person. Your opinions are worth listening to. Realize that you are an asset to your family and a valuable employee. Treat yourself that way. Remember the magic. If you believe that you are an important, worthwhile person, and begin to send those messages to the world you meet, it will change your life. ▪

Chapter 5

WHERE DO I BEGIN (TO ACCENTUATE THE POSITIVE)?

Maybe, just maybe, I'm on to something here. Maybe you do want to pay more attention to your clothes. Maybe you really want to develop a style of your own. It can be a daunting assignment, especially if you've spent the last few years trying not to think about your appearance, trying to wish yourself into invisibility. Now here I am telling you to come out of your shell! Create a personal style! Enjoy your clothes! Let your personality shine through each and every outfit.

But what does that mean? How do you get started on this journey?

Well, like any other trip, it begins with that all-important first step. And the song says it best: "Accentuate the positive! Eliminate the negative!" This may sound too simple to be important, but it is a powerful and significant concept. It's critical! It's all about focusing on your best features.

Yeah, right. Like you might have an attractive feature. Believe me, I know this can be hard. It certainly was a personal struggle for me. It was so difficult, as a matter of fact, that I actually had to write a little quiz to determine what about myself I hated the least. That's right: I couldn't think of a single thing about myself that I liked, so I set about choosing the thing I disliked the least. Pretty pathetic, eh?

But this really did help me to figure out, objectively, where I might start. So take a few minutes to fill in this little quiz. You might be pleasantly surprised. The important thing right now is that you try to be positive. Please don't rush through this and put a zero in every space. Work with me, girls....

The optimal frame of mind for you to be in during this quiz is honest and kind at the same time. Try to really separate each individual feature from the others as you score it.

WHAT DO I HATE THE LEAST?

We're scoring each feature here on a scale of zero to ten. That's right: consider each feature for a moment, and then assign it a number. If you love it, it's a ten. If you think it's the pits, give it a zero. Make yourself a nice cup of tea (coffee for me) and relax while you think about the Best of the Best! We're trying to be constructive here . . .

1. My hair is a

    0   1   2   3   4   5   6   7   8   9   10

2. My eyes are a

    0   1   2   3   4   5   6   7   8   9   10

3. My ears are a

    0   1   2   3   4   5   6   7   8   9   10

4. My nose is a

    0   1   2   3   4   5   6   7   8   9   10

5. My lips are a

    0   1   2   3   4   5   6   7   8   9   10

6. My teeth are a

    0   1   2   3   4   5   6   7   8   9   10

7. My chin is a

    0   1   2   3   4   5   6   7   8   9   10

8. My complexion is a

    0   1   2   3   4   5   6   7   8   9   10

9. My neck is a

    0   1   2   3   4   5   6   7   8   9   10

10. My bust is a

    0   1   2   3   4   5   6   7   8   9   10

11. My hands are a

    0   1   2   3   4   5   6   7   8   9   10

12. My fingernails are a

0   1   2   3   4   5   6   7   8   9   10

13. My upper arms are a

0   1   2   3   4   5   6   7   8   9   10

14. My wrists are a

0   1   2   3   4   5   6   7   8   9   10

15. My waist is a

0   1   2   3   4   5   6   7   8   9   10

16. My stomach is a

0   1   2   3   4   5   6   7   8   9   10

17. My hips are a

0   1   2   3   4   5   6   7   8   9   10

18. My butt is a

0   1   2   3   4   5   6   7   8   9   10

19. My thighs are a

0   1   2   3   4   5   6   7   8   9   10

20. My knees are a

0   1   2   3   4   5   6   7   8   9   10

21. My calves are a

0   1   2   3   4   5   6   7   8   9   10

22. My ankles are a

0   1   2   3   4   5   6   7   8   9   10

23. My feet are a

0   1   2   3   4   5   6   7   8   9   10

24. My toes are a

0   1   2   3   4   5   6   7   8   9   10

25. My smile is a

0   1   2   3   4   5   6   7   8   9   10

How'd you do? Any surprises? There is no total score here. We're just trying to determine which features you like the most.

When I took this little quiz, it quickly became apparent that I had very low self-esteem. I had a hard time thinking positively about myself at all. But when I reviewed my answers (nothing had scored higher than a six), I realized that my hair was my best feature. Tied with my smile. And I also thought my earlobes were fine—and my toes were damned near perfect. Wow! What a revelation. Something I didn't hate about myself. The truth is, I also liked my fingernails. I gave them a five.

So now what? Good question.

First of all, I'll share with you how this test affected me. It became the basis for my own personal style in a couple of interesting ways. Take the toe thing, for instance. I didn't even know I liked my feet! I went out and bought a great pair of hot pink shoes, with cute little cut-out designs on the top. That was the first time in a long time I'd spent money on myself. Shoes were a perfect, sort of non-

threatening thing to buy. Even though I'd gained a lot of weight, my feet were still the same size, and it was fun to go shoe shopping. So, it was a start.

But then what? Believe me when I tell you that at the time, there simply were no hot pink clothes available in size 22. (Rub a lamp!) I could have shopped for six months without finding a single thing! But don't forget: I sew! In fact: at that point, I owned a fabric store. So I made myself a dress exactly the way I wanted it.

My hair and fingernails were both a revelation to me, as well. I hadn't thought about it for years, but I was blessed with thick, dark, straight hair, and my fingernails were strong and attractive. Golly. I just used the word *attractive*. That's progress!

Here's the first outfit I ever made to go with those hot pink shoes. I loved this dress, and it was a big transition for me. The bright color, for one thing! I also loved the contrast created by color-blocking with the black fabric.

After taking stock of my newfound attributes, I decided to splurge on a great haircut and my first color job. I decided to get my first professional manicure, too. There is no way I can tell you what a big step this was for me.

I was feeling pretty terrific. Everybody loved my hair, and they were very complimentary about my wild new dress. I felt like Sally Field: "They like me! They really like me!" Sure enough, I found myself smiling more, experimenting with different colors and styles. As I started to look better, I was feeling better about myself. It was an amazing transformation. I went from basic black (and boring) to hot pink and orange overnight. Once I got started, nothing seemed too wild. The more outrageous it was, the more I liked it. It felt like I was getting in touch with the inner me for the first time in a long time. I know that sounds a little "California," especially coming from an Iowa farmgirl—but I loved these clothes! I was having a wonderful time. I didn't know it then, but I was changing more than my style. I was changing my life.

So let's think about this quiz, and how your answers might help you to find that all-important starting point. Remember, the idea here is to emphasize those things you like. Build on the positive. Make the most of your best features.

Let's say your ears are perfect. That's it! Time to go shopping for those terrific new show-stopping earrings. Yes. Start with the earrings. Focus on the earrings. Think about how great your earlobes are. Accent them. Concentrate on them. Let your lobes lead the way, girl! You will be amazed at how good this will feel. Once you've got earrings you love, put a matching outfit together.

Some things are obvious. If you have great legs—maybe you like your knees— then you should be directing your attention to finding or making some attractive skirts.

You might discover that your face is what you like the most. Time to hit the fancy makeup counter at one of those expensive department stores. (Maybe you'll get lucky, and Lancôme will be giving away a free gift that day!) Have a makeover. Did you know you can sit down, relax, and have a fabulous re-do? Sure, they're going to try to sell you something: that's their job. But they certainly don't expect every single person who sits down to buy into the entire line.

Then again, maybe you want to buy the whole line. I'm here to tell you that's perfectly OK. Or maybe you'll decide on a new tube of lipstick. So treat yourself. And don't ever forget that you also have the right to smile pleasantly, thank them for their time, and not buy a thing. I am empowering you to say no. They'll be fine. You'll survive. Nobody dies. Isn't it in the Constitution? Whenever you want to, you can say no. (This is really good to know, especially when those magazine solicitors call on the phone at suppertime.)

If your wrist is something you like: shop for some new watches or bracelets. Maybe you'll find a flashy new turquoise watch, and you'll have to make a southwestern outfit to go with it! Think cowboy boots….

When I realized that my fingernails were one of my better features, I not only got the manicure (now a regular treat), but I started buying rings for my fingers, too. That was fun. I discovered the ten-dollar "fashion" rings in department stores. Personally, I never cared whether something was "real" or not, anyway. The crystals looked as pretty as the diamonds did. (I'm sure my level of sophistication is showing!)

How much money I spent was not the issue. Accenting my finger with a pretty ring was the important thing—and it worked! People would comment all the time, and I realized that, by putting on some attractive jewelry, I was sending positive, cheerful, happy messages to the people I was meeting. They responded in kind. As people always do. I was changing myself. ▨

Part Two

STYLE VERSUS FASHION

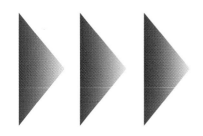

Chapter 6

BODY TYPES: WHICH ONE ARE YOU?

The best thing about developing your own style is that there are no right or wrong answers. It is a matter of personal taste. But after years of helping other women with patterns and fitting problems, I knew that what worked great for me wasn't necessarily the answer for every "gifted" woman. Because, although the problem is the same for all of us—FAT—it settles in different places, depending on your genetic make-up.

That's right…it's in the genes. There are three different fat genes:

❖ The all-over fat gene
❖ The top-heavy fat gene
❖ The bottom-heavy fat gene

If I owned a university, I'm sure I could commission a study that would support my three-gene theory. However, in lieu of a university study, try looking around the next time you're at a family reunion. Blue eyes run in families, red hair is common to some other families, and big butts can definitely be an inherited trait. Trust me.

There are three basic body shapes.

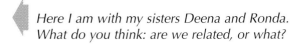

Here I am with my sisters Deena and Ronda. What do you think: are we related, or what?

Rubenesque

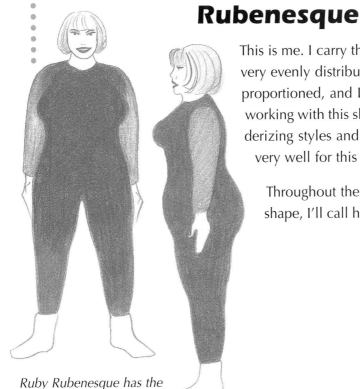

This is me. I carry the extra weight all over my body; it's very evenly distributed. The good news is that I'm well-proportioned, and I have a definite waistline. I've been working with this shape for years, and many of the slenderizing styles and solutions to fashion problems work very well for this body.

Throughout the book, if I need to refer to this body shape, I'll call her Ruby, short for Ruby Rubenesque.

Ruby Rubenesque has the all-over fat gene.

Wineglass-Shaped

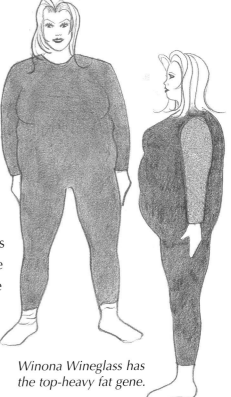

This woman carries all her weight up front and on top, in her bodice, midriff, and stomach. She often has no butt at all, and very skinny legs. My lovely mother-in-law, Helen, is four foot eleven and has this shape; so does Roseanne. If you are this body type, you know it. This woman can never buy a pants suit to fit, because she's so top-heavy. If the jacket is big enough, she'll be swimming in the skirt or pants that go with the suit. Sound familiar?

I'll call this woman Winona, short for Winona Wineglass.

Winona Wineglass has the top-heavy fat gene.

Christmas-Tree-Shaped

This is the most challenging body shape to work with. Quite the opposite of Winona, this woman is bottom-heavy. She has narrow shoulders, often with a proportionately small bust. Her biggest problem is usually her derriere and hips. Her legs can be very heavy. If a dress fits her in the hips, the shoulder seams are down around her elbows. Do you know her?

I'm going to call this lady Christina, short for Christina Christmas Tree.

Christina Christmas Tree has the bottom-heavy fat gene.

My hope is that after reading these three simple body-type descriptions, you'll have a general idea of which one you are. Ruby is a classic shape and comprises about 50% of the gifted women in America. The rest of the gifted women are split pretty evenly between Winona and Christina, each of whom accounts for about 25%.

Making the Most of It

Don't be worried if you're not sure which "category" you fall into. These are not hard and fast definitions. If you're not sure whether you're a Ruby or a Winona, maybe I can help. A belt could be the determining factor. Put one on right now. Walk around the house. If the belt stays in place, you're most likely a Ruby. If it flips up into your boobs, you're probably a Winona.

You might be a Ruby with Christina characteristics. This is not a good thing or a bad thing. Please don't be intimidated by this body-type information. It's offered here to give you some general guidelines.

The important thing to believe is that, no matter what body shape you are, it's right for you. Honest. This is the hand we were dealt, girls. The important thing is to make the most of it. Let's learn how to accent the best of each different type, and camouflage the negative. We're going to spend our time working to minimize our flaws and maximize our best features.

So our bodies aren't perfect. Who really cares? What's the point of perfect, anyway? Who gets to define perfect? Perfect is just a fantasy ideal—dreamed up by some Madison Avenue executive. What a genius that guy was! He can use perfect to sell us more shampoo and cosmetics. Perfect will get us to spend money on products we really don't need. Perfect is something we never will be, no matter how hard we try, how long we diet, how much we exercise, or how much we weigh. Perfect is something we're supposed to aspire to, in order to make them rich.

Don't you see? Perfect is not a good thing. Perfect is a weapon they use against us. Do not be fooled. What would be the point of perfect? Think about that for a minute. If you are the perfect size, does that mean you'll be happy? If you have the perfect body, does that mean you're a better person? A more loving wife? A more caring mother? A more efficient worker? Could you be a better friend? Is perfect something that matters? To whom?

I am not happy with my body. I do not like being this fat. I do not think I'm beautiful. Certainly I know I'm not perfect.

But I have accepted imperfect. I know that I do my best every single day. For me, it's no longer just about the weight. My life is more than that. I am more than that. My value is not determined by my size. Yours isn't either. Don't let yourself believe that it is.

I loved the movie *The Sound of Music.* I recently watched it again, after twenty years, and was surprised by the message the Reverend Mother gave to Maria. (Maria was afraid that falling in love with her boss would get in the way of her becoming a nun.) It was so simple: "You must find your own life."

So that is our mission. Not to be perfect. But to be the best that we can be. (Why does everything sound like an Army slogan?) Right now. This minute. To use our clothes to our best advantage. To build our confidence and enthusiasm by creating a personal style we are comfortable with.

Maybe you don't think you can do this. Maybe you're afraid you'll fail. Are you getting a pit in your stomach? Does the idea of spending money on new clothes terrify you? That's a good thing. Remember, we must do those things we are most afraid of. I always tell my boys that there is no shame in failure. The only real failure is in not trying. Who was it who said: "If you begin an important endeavor, there is a chance of failure. If you do not begin, your failure is certain."

Chapter 7

HOW IMPORTANT IS FIT?

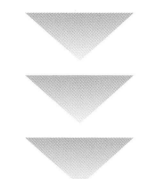

Never underestimate the importance of proper fit.

Fit is it!

It's just that simple. A clarifying moment for me was the day I walked into Kmart behind a very large woman who was wearing a pair of pull-on polyester pants that were way too tight. The pants were riding down in the back and clinging to every cellulite dimple. That was the only thing I noticed about that woman. In my mind, "Dimple Butt" became the enemy. I made a silent resolution at that moment to check my derriere every time I left my house. No tight pants for me!

If your clothes do not fit properly, nothing else matters. No one will notice your beautiful suit. They won't see the expensive fabric or the fine workmanship. They will not for one minute think about how much money you might have paid for that great outfit. Because they will only see your Dimple Butt. We are all judged. Remember the three-second rule. That very important first impression happens almost before you can blink.

If you don't believe me, try this: go to your local mall and sit on a bench for an hour. Take note of the people who walk by, and as they pass, write down your first impression of each one. Believe me: what you'll notice will be the negative things. And the people you will judge most harshly will be the ones who left the house wearing shapeless, too-tight pants.

Don't be that woman in the too-tight pants. Nobody can make you go out of your house in clothes that don't fit. Please buy or make something for yourself that will fit you right now. How long has it been? Are you trying to make do with your current tired old clothes because you're hoping to be a smaller size in the near future?

Snap out of it!

Remember when Cher said that in *Moonstruck*?

We are certainly all guilty of this to one extent or another. We don't like our weight, we're unhappy with our size; so we won't buy anything until we lose the weight. I've heard heartbreaking stories about women who refuse to shop until they lose weight. One woman was shopping for a dress for her son's wedding. For months, she would try on clothes and say, "No, I'm not going to buy anything yet, because I want to get down to a smaller size." One morning she walked in and said "What do you have in light blue? The wedding is today at four."

Cheryl Groth is a District Manager for Catherine's, a chain specializing in clothes for gifted women. She sees hundreds of women every week in stores all over the Midwest. She says: "Women are too hard on themselves. They worry about what size something is, often refusing to move into a larger size, instead telling themselves they must lose weight. That means they're wearing clothes that are too tight, and often outdated."

So: how to snap out of it? Again, you need to start someplace. Choose a few basic articles of clothing. Keep in mind constraints such as your lifestyle and your comfort zone. If you go to work in an office every day, you may prefer separates or dresses. If you have a more casual lifestyle, you might live in jeans and sweatshirts. Here's a little quiz to help you think about your preferences.

WHAT CLOTHES WORK FOR YOU?

You know the drill. Score from zero (awful) to ten (great).

1. When I'm wearing knit pants, I feel

0   1   2   3   4   5   6   7   8   9   10

2. When I'm wearing blue jeans, I feel

0   1   2   3   4   5   6   7   8   9   10

3. When I'm wearing a dress, I feel

0   1   2   3   4   5   6   7   8   9   10

4. When I'm wearing a long jacket, I feel

    0   1   2   3   4   5   6   7   8   9   10

5. When I'm wearing a long skirt, I feel

    0   1   2   3   4   5   6   7   8   9   10

6. When I'm wearing a tight skirt, I feel

    0   1   2   3   4   5   6   7   8   9   10

7. When I'm wearing a great suit, I feel

    0   1   2   3   4   5   6   7   8   9   10

8. When I'm wearing a big sweatshirt, I feel

    0   1   2   3   4   5   6   7   8   9   10

9. When I'm wearing a turtleneck, I feel

    0   1   2   3   4   5   6   7   8   9   10

10. When I'm wearing a silk blouse, I feel

    0   1   2   3   4   5   6   7   8   9   10

11. When I'm wearing a bulky sweater, I feel

    0   1   2   3   4   5   6   7   8   9   10

12. When I'm naked, I feel

    0   1   2   3   4   5   6   7   8   9   10

Maybe you should be a stripper. See how revealing these little quizzes can be? It's time you learned something about the inner you.

In this day and age, of course, we must think about our work situations as well. So think about what clothes your job dictates to you. Do you have to wear business suits? Sunday-best dresses? Separates: skirts, pants, and jackets? Or is your work very casual—can you get away with wearing denim?

Now think about where the overlap is between the clothes that make you feel good and the clothes you need to wear for work. Once you have determined the kind of clothes that will fit into your lifestyle and work situation, it's time to go shopping!

Unfortunately, when you go, there are a couple of pitfalls to watch out for. Let me tell you what they are, and what to look for when you're shopping.

Common Fitting Problems

It doesn't matter whether you sew your own clothes or buy them off the rack, you're going to run into two common fitting problems: the dinner-plate neckline and the dropped shoulder seam. Most pattern companies do not understand our bodies. Neither do the clothing manufacturers. I'm going to explain why these two problems happen over and over again.

Clothing manufacturers and pattern companies seem to believe that if a woman is size 16 or up, her neck exploded and her shoulders blew up. How many times have you seen a gifted woman wearing a top with a huge, gappy neckline—and shoulder seams down around her elbows?

Both fitting problems are caused by the same recurring pattern mistake. A typical blouse pattern is half a front. It becomes a whole front when they place the half-pattern piece on the fold of the fabric, and cut it out. This has served the industry well for over a hundred years. And it makes sense for lots of reasons. For one, it's much easier to keep the fabric straight and on-grain that way. Also, by cutting the front piece folded at the center front line, both armhole openings will be cut at the same time, and more likely will be identical.

Large-sized clothes too often don't fit gifted women. Notice where the shoulder seams are (how low can you go!) and how the neckline gapes.

However, our fitting problems occur when they use this half-pattern method to size "up" for a gifted woman. The easiest thing to do is to move the pattern piece one inch away from the fold of the fabric, and then cut. This adds four inches into the body of the shirt. Perfect, right?

Wrong. Adjusting the pattern that way means that every single shirt, blouse, top, or dress will have a gappy dinner-plate neckline, and the sleeve seams meant to be on top of our shoulders will end up down near our elbows.

This problem is then exaggerated by the fact that the models for large-sized clothes are always size 14. That's what looks good on the runway. Isn't that bogus? So when the necklines are wrong and huge and gappy,

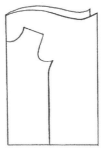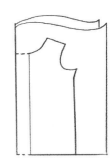

Here you see the half-pattern for a size 14 shirt front. In the second drawing, they just set the pattern away from the fold line before they cut. Yes, it adds fabric in the body (where we need it), but it also makes for a much bigger neck opening, and the shoulder seams will now be in all the wrong places.

the designers convince themselves it's only because the model isn't really big enough. Trust me: Godzilla's neck would not be big enough!

You gotta wonder if they ever put these clothes on the people who are supposed to wear them! The truth is, I have bought (and made) many tops that would have been too big in the shoulders for Arnold Schwarzenegger. (Although, come to think of it, the enormous gappy neck opening might have been about right for the Terminator.)

Finding or Making Clothes That Fit Anyway

Here's the deal. If you sew, you can do whatever you want with the pattern. Obviously, adjusting patterns is no easy thing. But my dear friend Phyllis Krogman (also a lovely gifted lady) helped me to create the "perfect" pattern for my body. The adjustment is based on some simple, easy-to-understand fitting principles, and you'll find it described in the Bonus Sewing Section at the end of this book. Even if you don't sew, there are some basics of good fit you should know.

First of all, no matter which figure type you are—Ruby, Winona, or Christina—you carry your weight below your armpits. Am I right? This piece of information is an incredible fitting breakthrough. We complain because we put on weight in our midriff, or in our stomach, or in our hips. That's the Big Three. Midriff; Stomach; Hips. Sound familiar? Not one woman, anyplace in the country, has complained to me that her biggest figure problem is her shoulder area!

Therefore, shoulder pads are an essential part of our wardrobe. They help to give us balance. This is critically important! Shoulder pads define our shoulders and put our entire body into proportion. Adding the right shoulder pads can make you look like you lost fifteen pounds. It's really amazing. (Maybe if I wear four pair it'll look like I lost 60 pounds!)

Think of it this way: my sister Ronda is a size 14 and I'm a size 24, but if you compare our shoulder-to-shoulder measurement (across the back), hers is sixteen inches and mine is sixteen and a half! Get it? We don't gain weight in our shoulders. We gain the weight below our armpits, and we need the shoulder pads to make everything look more proportionate.

See how shoulder pads balance the proportions of this Ruby-shaped woman.

So if you're shopping for clothes, remember to look carefully at several things. First and foremost, make sure the shoulder seams actually sit on your shoulders and the neckline fits you properly. Obviously, you also want clothes that are comfortable, that zip and button easily, and that don't tug or pull when you move around.

Take the time to make sure that the clothes fit you right in all of these ways. (In chapter 8, I also give some specific tips about how to make sure pants will fit.) And never, ever buy anything that is too small, hoping you'll lose weight!

The most important thing to remember is that nobody cares what size you wear! Get over it! The number on the tag doesn't matter to anyone but you.

Look for necklines that fit well and shoulder seams that actually sit on your shoulders.

Chapter 8

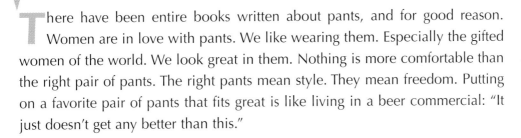

PANTS: A DREAM COME TRUE, OR A NIGHTMARE?

There have been entire books written about pants, and for good reason. Women are in love with pants. We like wearing them. Especially the gifted women of the world. We look great in them. Nothing is more comfortable than the right pair of pants. The right pants mean style. They mean freedom. Putting on a favorite pair of pants that fits great is like living in a beer commercial: "It just doesn't get any better than this."

However, getting pants to fit right can be a very frustrating endeavor. No two behinds are alike. (Of course, it would be a pretty dreary world if we all had the same body. Just imagine millions of women who look like Claudia Schiffer. Boring, eh? Work with me here...) And for us gifted women, pants can be an extra challenge, no doubt about it. But they're well worth the effort. The trick is to figure out which pants work best on your body.

Believe me: there's a pants possibility for every gifted woman. However, buying or sewing pants that fit properly can be a huge problem in itself. While doing research for this book, most of the women I surveyed listed "pants that fit" as a major priority. (Of course, I do think sewing them is the best solution: in ten years, I have helped hundreds of women sew pants that fit their bodies.)

The first order of business is to discuss four different styles of pants that work extremely well for the gifted woman.

1. Basic Pants

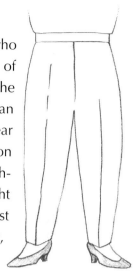

Is there a woman in the world who hasn't worn these pants? Think of them as the Type O blood group (the universal blood type; everyone can take it). Every body type can wear basic pants. They come in pull-on style or with a zipper, with or without pockets, with narrow or straight pant legs. The fabric can be just about anything: cotton, rayon, knit, or denim. These pants can be a dressy trouser with pleats or a simple pair of blue jeans.

Basic pants.

Kim is ready to go in her basic print pants, combined with a solid top.

2. Stirrup Pants

Because I am such a fan of stirrup pants, I live in fear that one day soon they will go out of fashion. However, in doing research for this book, I discovered that I am not their only fan! According to Mary Richardson, Marketing Director of Lane Bryant, the largest

Deena and Beth both look great in checked stirrup pants!

retail chain catering to the gifted woman, stirrups are selling very well. Even after five years in the forefront, these pants are still being shipped by the truckload every week. When it comes to pants, I think we have to go back to the concept of style (your own lasting style) versus fashion (the fad of the moment). What we're concerned about is whether or not they look good on you. That's the only important thing.

Stirrup pants.

3. Harem Pants

Harem pants are currently not in vogue. Too bad! Because I simply can't write about pants without talking about this wonderful, flattering style. Fortunately, though, everything cycles in the fashion world, so I'm confident they'll make a comeback. These pants are cut with an extremely full seat, and often an extended crotch, with wide, easy-fitting upper legs. The key element in the harem pants is that they narrow substantially at the ankle. This makes for a very flattering look (Christina Christmas Tree looks especially fabulous in these).

Harem pants.

Harem pants are best in a soft, drapable fabric. They're great in rayon, crinkle cotton, silk, or knit fabrics.

Julie, I love that belt and necklace with your teal harem pants.

4. Palazzo Pants

In the last forty years, palazzo pants have come and gone on the fashion scene. These pants are a classic (again: think style, not fashion!). I wore my first pair of palazzo pants in 1973, and I've been a fan ever since. Don't con-

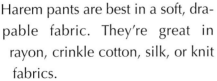

Palazzo pants.

Palazzo pants: an especially good option for a dress-up occasion. Don't we look hot?

fuse these with bell bottoms: the difference is that the palazzo pants have a loose seat, and as the pants drape, they can look like a long skirt. Sometimes it won't even become apparent that you're wearing pants until you walk. These pants are timeless and a great option for those dressy occasions.

Making Them Fit

When it comes to pants, choosing the right style is only the first step. The real challenge is getting them to fit your body. So let's talk about the correct fit. What specific things should you be looking for? When I'm shopping for pants, I always do the following three tests.

The pull-on test

If I have to struggle to pull them on, they go right back on the rack. It's just that simple.

Don't buy pants if you can't pull them on easily.

The bend-over test

After I have them on, I bend over and touch my toes (well, sort of). What I'm looking for here is the ride-down factor. I don't want the back waist of the pants to pull down.

The sit-down test

This is important. Sitting down will move the stress to a different place. It's often at this point that I feel the back waist of the pants starting to pull down. Because your hips spread when you sit down, this test will often illustrate that the pants are too tight in the upper legs. If I have to tug the pants legs back down when I stand up, the pants don't fit.

Use the bend-over test to avoid that "construction worker" low-rider look.

Don't neglect the sit-down test: your pants are stretched in different ways when you sit.

These three tests might seem too simple to you. The truth is, women have a tendency to force things when it comes to pants. We kid ourselves into believing that if we can just get them zipped, it'll be all right. Forget about it! Pants are like men that way: if you have any doubt at all in the very beginning, take a pass. Otherwise, you'll only regret it.

Always remember that all you're looking for is pants that fit your body; you don't care in the least what "size" they are. Clothing manufacturers have made a real effort to standardize sizes, but sizing still remains a mystery. So don't worry about it! If you have to buy a bigger size to get the pants big enough in the hip area, just do it. The fit is the important thing, not the size number on the tag. If your pants look good on you, and fit well, you'll soon forget what size they are. It doesn't matter!

I wish I could get women to believe that. The fit is what's important, not the size.

Do I sound like a broken record yet? We get all hung up on this size thing. Cheryl Groth of Catherine's sees it every day in her job. I see it in hundreds of responses to my self-image quiz. Women refuse to buy new clothes that are one size larger. We believe that buying a bigger size is admitting failure. We torture ourselves. But for what? When was the last time you walked up to a friend or acquaintance and said "Gee, that dress looks great on you—what size is it?" I'm willing to bet that's never happened. But how about the last time you saw a gifted woman wearing skintight pants? You thought, "Boy, look at those bulges. She looks like she swallowed a Pontiac." Am I right?

And remember: shopping for pants that fit can be a challenge. But how about sewing pants? Many women believe it would be easier to nail Jell-O to a tree. Well, like most things, we tend to overthink it. It's not such a big deal. Even if you've had a bad experience in the past, maybe sworn off sewing pants forever: give it one more chance! I think it's worth the effort. If you want to give it another try, I give you some suggestions in the Bonus Sewing Section in the back of this book. ▨

Chapter 9

WHICH STYLES ARE BEST ON WHICH BODY TYPES?

Ruby Rubenesque

If she had been born in France two hundred years ago, Ruby would have been revered and worshiped. Her zaftig, full-figured body would have been the envy of every poor, lonely, unattractive, skinny woman in Europe, and she would have been in demand to pose naked for all the finest artists.

This body type has certain real advantages. The best thing about Ruby is that she is well proportioned. She is often five-foot-five or taller, which is another good thing. She has a lovely bustline and sometimes a well-defined waistline (although Ruby may also have a straight up-and-down shape, with no discernible waist). She usually has shapely legs, with nice ankles.

Some of Ruby's Most Flattering Styles

Pants

Ruby got lucky here. Of the four pants styles we discussed, she can wear them all! She looks good in pants and she knows it. The basic pants are great, and the stirrup pants can be wonderful. She also looks good in the harem pants,

Callie has that well-proportioned Ruby Rubenesque shape.

Lucky Ruby Rubenesque: she can wear all pants styles and look great.

Lisa is a statuesque Ruby in her striped basic pants.

and the palazzo pants are perfect for a change of pace or dressier look. Ruby's well-proportioned body was made for pants. She should wear them often because she wears them very well.

Tops

Ruby may prefer the mock turtleneck style, depending on her individual double chin factor. She often tucks in her tops and looks great in a belt. Any blouse type will work for her, and necklines are largely a matter of her personal taste. Much will depend on the jewelry or accessories she is attracted to.

Remember the twin pitfalls of dinner-plate neckline and dropped shoulder seams! Ruby, when you shop, look for shoulder seams that fall right at your shoulders and avoid getting tops with those gappy neck openings. It's generally best to avoid anything sleeveless. Nobody has seen *my* flabby upper arms since 1973.

Mock turtlenecks and all shapes of necklines work well for Ruby.

Skirts

Ruby has a number of choices in skirts. She can wear a straight skirt or a gored skirt. She also looks great in a trumpet skirt, and pleats work fine as well. Although flat pleats are an option, remember the boxed pleated skirts that had the pleats sewn down six inches or so from the waistband? Although currently not in vogue, that skirt still looks good on Ruby.

As for the all-important question of hemlines, Ruby's best choice is a hemline right at her knee or anywhere below, all the way down to her ankle.

The gored skirt and the tiered skirt widen as they go down and add to Ruby's long vertical line.

Ronda loved the flowers on this long skirt so much she planted some on her top.

ONE IMPORTANT SKIRT TIP

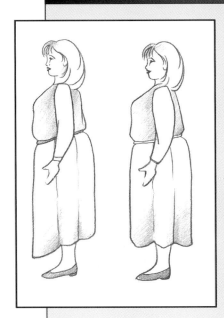

Ruby's waistline is often sloped, lower in the front and higher in the back, so that her hemline also hangs lower in the front than the back. Bummer! Sometimes this can be such a problem that Ruby will regretfully stay away from skirts altogether. Making an alteration can be difficult and time-consuming, so my fitting tip is simply to roll the waistband only *in the front.* Honest: I'm an accomplished seamstress, and yet I do this all the time! Because I often wear belts, nobody even notices that I "rolled" (sounds like some shady drug practice, doesn't it?).

Ruby can fix her sloped-waist problem with a simple roll of the waistband in the front.

Jackets

Jackets are very important for Ruby. Nothing adds a vertical line more quickly than a jacket. Wearing the jacket open allows Ruby to expose a belt buckle or other decorative motif that can add interest to her outfit. The best part of the open-jacket outfit for Ruby is that only four inches of her waist are visible. Even if her waist isn't particularly small or well defined, she's now created a wonderful optical illusion—a four-inch waist. Pretty cool. Ruby has a wide range of jacket styles to choose from. The classic blazer is good. Depending on her personal taste, she might prefer a more unconstructed look. Even a long sweater can accomplish great things for Ruby.

The jacket is often a place where Ruby can hike up her color quotient. It's amazing how great a simple purple jacket worn over plain black pants and a top can be. Never underestimate the power of a good jacket. Think about the way men dress: isn't it always the detail of a good suit jacket that makes an impression?

Ruby in her classic blazer: very smart and vertical, vertical, vertical.

For Ruby, the swing jacket is a very flattering style, because it does a great job of accentuating the positive while disguising the negative. She always needs to consider her personal taste in color and details, of course, but she ought to be attracted to the longer length: she looks great in it! Ruby, the jacket hem should be at least as far down as your fingertips reach; try the duster length, too.

Deena and Callie accentuate their striking Ruby looks with colorful swing jackets.

Molli Rae looks great in this simple black sheath with an outrageous necklace.

Ruby can happily belt her dresses to accentuate that waistline; as with separates, she needs to make sure that all the fitting details are just right.

Dresses

Because she is well-proportioned, Ruby looks great in a dress. I love the simple style of a knit dress with a fitted top, a defined waistline, and a gored skirt. She can look wonderful in a proper sheath dress or a simple shirtwaist. If Ruby is short-waisted, she may not be able to wear a belt. In that case, the sheath dress can be a great choice because it avoids the waist issue.

The same general rules that apply to separates apply here as well: make sure the sleeves aren't too tight, the fabric has a nice drape to it, and the hemline falls between your knees and ankles.

Ruby can get a lot of mileage out of a basic dress by adding jackets and accessories.

Biggest Mistakes Ruby Can Make

Wearing Clothes Too Tight

This is always a major mistake. It's very unattractive, and it always calls attention to problem areas. Did you ever walk behind a woman whose body rolls tood out, individually, and you wanted to count them? Bad, bad, bad….

Don't do it, Ruby! Wear something that fits you right!

Banded Tops

OK, this is a qualified mistake. If Ruby pulls the top down and the banded bottom pulls right across her tummy, she's emphasizing what is not usually her best feature. These tops are meant to be worn loosely, with the band sitting right on top of the hips, creating a blousy effect. A top like this can actually work fine, but Ruby has to make sure she's wearing it right.

Thong Bikinis

Yeah, right....

Winona Wineglass

The best thing about Winona is that she has skinny legs and, often, no butt at all! So these are the features she should emphasize.

Because Winona is top-heavy, she carries the extra weight in her midriff and tummy, so that is her special challenge when she is trying to find clothes that fit. To add to the challenge, she is often short. (I'm sorry, I can't say "vertically challenged"! I think it's so silly. Winona, I hope you don't mind me calling you short.)

Some of Winona's Most Flattering Styles

Pants

Two pants styles out of the four we've talked about will work for Winona. First of all, the basic pants can look very good on Winona. But, better yet, she looks absolutely terrific in the stirrup

Beth has the Winona Wineglass advantage: she can show off her skinny legs whenever she wants!

pants! They were designed with her figure in mind, and they focus on her very best feature, those skinny, good-looking legs. Remember, accentuate the positive, eliminate the negative.

And as an added bonus, Winona can and should wear shorts! In my opinion, this is the biggest advantage Winona has: she looks great in shorts, and she ought to flaunt those wonderful legs. Also, because she is often short, she'll want to keep in mind that the more leg she manages to show, the taller she will look.

These are the pants that look best on Winona: basic pants, stirrup pants, and shorts give her a chance to show some leg.

Tops

Winona can be very busty, often without a defined waistline, so choosing the right tops can be a challenge. She looks best in a loose-fitting, flowing style. "Long over lean" was invented with Winona in mind (long over lean means a long top worn out, not tucked in, to top off close-fitting or "lean" pants such as Capris, leggings, or stirrup pants). She will definitely not want to tuck in her tops.

The fabric of Winona's tops can be as important as the style. She should select fabrics that drape and flow.

Winona often has very slender hips. That's why the dolman look—full in the bosom, but close-fitting at

Tina in stirrup pants under a long, flowing top.

the hips—is very good on her. Because it has no defined shoulder seam, she doesn't have to worry about the seam falling off her shoulders. Necklines, again, are a matter of her personal taste.

Loose-fitting tops in fabrics that drape and flow are the best for Winona.

Skirts

Of all our sisters, Winona Wineglass is the one who can get away with a straight mini-skirt! This is the best thing she has going for her. Hurray for her: she has those great skinny legs, usually with perfect kneecaps, and she ought to flaunt them. Remember, accentuate the positive….

Winona needs to go for a shorter hemline. Although she looks great in a straight skirt, she can also choose a softly gathered short skirt, or even a trumpet skirt, always remembering to show as much leg as possible. Winona will almost always have to shorten whatever she buys.

Winona is the one gifted sister who gets to wear those short, short skirts!

63

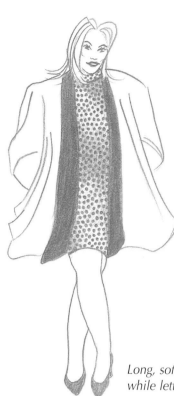

Jackets

With jackets, again, think long over lean. Soft, unconstructed styles will be best. Winona needs to make sure that when she stands with her arms at her side, her jacket goes down at least to her fingertips. Again, she will want to select fabrics that drape and flow.

When Winona wears her jackets open, exposing the blouse underneath, she creates a good vertical line: that is very important in slenderizing her upper body.

Dresses

Because Winona is larger on the top than on the bottom, finding a dress that fits her correctly can be difficult. She doesn't want anything fitted at the waist, but a sheath style will look great on

Long, soft, and flowing jackets work well on Winona while letting her show off those legs once again!

A sheath dress looks great on either a Ruby or a Winona.

her. Another good choice is the bubble dress. This style has a dropped waistline, with the skirt often attached to an underslip. The bubble dress can be a very comfortable, attractive style for Winona, and the dropped waistline is particularly good on her.

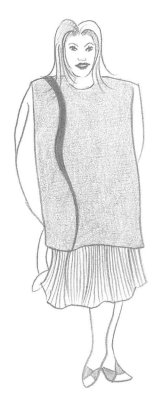

A dropped waistline looks particularly good on Winona's wineglass shape.

Biggest Mistakes Winona Can Make

Wearing a belt

Every time Winona tries to wear a belt, it rides up under her bustline. The styles that look best on Winona completely ignore her waist. My mother-in-law once told me that she got sick of me always talking about wearing a belt. She said that when she tried it, her boobs were the only thing that kept the belt from choking her!

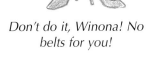

Don't do it, Winona! No belts for you!

Short or banded tops

The ribbed band will emphasize Winona's tummy. The short tops stop right where she does not want to draw attention—this is not a good thing.

Christina Christmas Tree

Whereas Winona Wineglass is top-heavy, Christina Christmas Tree is bottom-heavy. She carries most of her weight below her waistline. Christina tells me she hates her butt, and she is the woman, wherever I go, who refers to her upper legs as thunder thighs. She carries a lot of her weight in her legs and even her ankles can be a problem. Because her top is often the smallest part of her body, we must find ways to emphasize it and blend it in with her bottom.

Some of Christina's Most Flattering Styles

Pants

Three of the four pants styles we've talked about are especially good for Christina. First of all, the harem pants are designed specifically with her figure type in mind. She looks great in these! They're cut with a very full seat and thigh, yet they narrow at the ankle. This is one of those styles that comes and goes in retail ready-to-wear, but as far as I'm concerned, it's a classic.

The harem pants are best in a soft, flowing fabric, which is also the fabric Christina is looking for in palazzo pants. These pants are wonderful for Christina. They should be full-cut, and the legs should get wider and wider until at the bottom the leg has a twenty-five to thirty-inch opening. Palazzo pants are an especially good choice for evening wear.

Julie stepping out in purple: these palazzo pants are a classy option for the Christina Christmas Tree shape.

Christina in soft, flowing pants: harem or palazzo. Notice how she gets to draw attention to the small top half of her body.

Christina can also wear basic pants. Finding basic pants or jeans that fit properly can be a challenge for Christina, though. Often, if the pants fit in the hips, they'll be too big in the waist.

Tops

This is Christina's finest feature, and the tops she chooses are crucial. Believe it or not, Christina should tuck in her top. This helps to emphasize her often small waistline, and keeps the focus on her upper body, the smallest part of her. Also, if she tries to wear a top out, it will often pull across her hips or, even worse, ride up!

Again, I believe necklines to be a personal choice. While some might prefer turtlenecks, the rest would choose a button-down-the-front blouse. No matter what top or blouse Christina chooses, shoulder pads are a must. It is especially important that she take advantage of those wonderful foam pads that will provide balance to her body.

Christina looks great in a banded top, but it's important that she wear it properly. The band must sit on the top of her hips, not pulled across her stomach. That way, the top itself blousons. This is an effective way to blend her smaller top with her bigger bottom.

Christina keeps the focus on her upper body by tucking in her top or by wearing a banded top that makes her top look larger with its blousoning effect.

Skirts

Skirts are very important and comfortable for Christina. The style she looks best in starts off close-fitting at her waist and gets wider as it drops—a gored skirt of soft-flowing fabric, for example. Maybe a broomstick or peasant-style skirt. The tiered skirt is great for her as well. Her skirts should always gain fabric "width" as they drop. That means she will be emphasizing her best feature— her small waist. She will prefer a longer length. Certainly below the knee. She might even like her skirts ankle length. Remember, it's about personal style, not trendy fashion.

Christina looks great in a long, flowing broomstick or peasant skirt. Her hemline is definitely below the knees. Skirts are best out of soft, flowing fabric that will drape. Christina looks great in a split skirt, too.

Lucky Christina has lots of options in skirts; they're best in soft, draping fabrics.

Jackets

Here's the problem with jackets. Consider a basic blazer: by the time Christina buys it big enough for her hips, the shoulders and neckline are way too big and baggy for her. And, if she buys it to fit her shoulders, it will pull open at her hips, emphasizing her worst figure problem. One of the best looks for her is a jacket that comes just to the top of her hips. This is a real help in blending her top and bottom. She should wear the jacket open, exposing the contrasting blouse, thus creating a good vertical line. Christina also looks great in a short vest, which not

Christina looks great in a short jacket or short vest. If she really wants something long, she should make it a swing coat.

only adds those vertical lines but also does a great job of gracefully blending her top and bottom.

The only long jacket I'd recommend for Christina is a swing coat. My favorite, of course, is Rita's Coat (designed by me, Rita Farro, and available as Pattern #535 from the Stretch & Sew Pattern Company). Because of the dolman sleeve design, this swing coat is a great look on all three body types, and especially good for Christina.

Tina chose a shorter, color-blocked jacket to go with her long skirt.

You just gotta have one good dress. The red plaid is actually a separate jacket over a "slip dress."

Dresses

Christina is thinking: oh no, not another version of the float dress! Well, it's true enough that the float is a very nice style for her body, but it isn't her only choice. There's something new: the slip dress. It's a little tricky. Inside, the skirt is sewn onto a simple slip top. The actual bodice of the dress is often a separate piece. The jacket sits right at the top of the hips.

Christina looks great in a float dress, but if she wants a little variety she can try a slip dress.

I don't have to explain why this jacket that fits at the shoulders but not at the hips is a bad idea for Christina.

Biggest Mistake Christina Can Make

Clothes that are too tight

Because her hips are bigger, Christina often ends up in pants that are too tight. Remember, get over the size thing. Make sure your clothes fit properly and are comfortable.

One very common mistake Christina makes is to wear a long jacket. She's trying to cover her hips. However, if the jacket fits her in the shoulders, it will be pulling tightly across her hips. This greatly emphasizes her worst feature.

Your Own Personal Style

Please trust your own taste. Don't lose sight of the main point here: developing your own personal style. You should experiment and choose clothes that you feel comfortable in and that reflect your personality. Again, not every woman will fit neatly into one of these three body types. These illustrations and photographs are supposed to give you some new ideas—maybe provide a little inspiration!

Remember: take advantage of those first three seconds. That's the important thing. The best defense is always a good offense. ▪

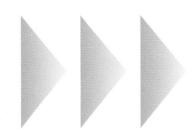

Chapter 10

OPTICAL ILLUSIONS: COLOR BLOCKING AND THE ALL-IMPORTANT VERTICAL LINE

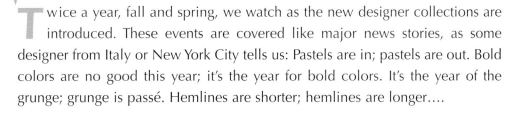

Twice a year, fall and spring, we watch as the new designer collections are introduced. These events are covered like major news stories, as some designer from Italy or New York City tells us: Pastels are in; pastels are out. Bold colors are no good this year; it's the year for bold colors. It's the year of the grunge; grunge is passé. Hemlines are shorter; hemlines are longer....

Forget about them! I can't remember ever seeing a single garment on a single model walking down a runway that applied to my life. As I was working on this book, the Paris spring shows were featuring women wearing jackets open in the front, with no blouse at all. Gee, that's bound to catch on. Remember the difference between fashion and style: fashion is trendy and faddish, whereas style is about classic choices that will stand the test of time. Style is about what looks good on us. Fashion is a cheap white plastic chair; style is a classic wicker rocker. Fashion is the rebel you fell madly in love with in high school. Maybe the relationship burned like a comet, but it couldn't last. Style is the hardworking, steady guy you married who knows how to fix dishwashers and mow the grass.

We have the right to ignore the so-called fashion gurus. We have no need to be intimidated by them. We cannot give in to the tyranny of the fashion industry.

 Kim in a color-blocked suit.

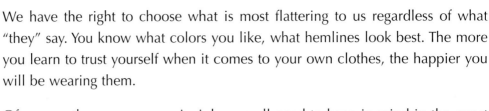

We have the right to choose what is most flattering to us regardless of what "they" say. You know what colors you like, what hemlines look best. The more you learn to trust yourself when it comes to your own clothes, the happier you will be wearing them.

Of course, there are some principles we all need to keep in mind in the quest for our own very personal style.

The Vertical Line

The importance of the vertical line is a major principle for the gifted women of the world. It is as important to us as the law of gravity is to an egg. Just remember:

> **Up and down—not round and round.**

And how do we get those vertical lines? Ever heard of color blocking? Well, you're about to get a crash course in the subtle art of body division. By adding vertical lines, you divide your body and subtract pounds. It's an optical illusion. It works every time. It's magic: instant weight loss without liposuction!

Color is an enormously important tool in working with our wardrobe. Whether you're shopping or sewing your clothes, color should always be a major consideration, but it's one that we often ignore. If you're overweight and unhappy about how you look in clothes, you may be wearing dark colors, trying to look invisible. Do not be a prisoner to black! Free yourself, girls: you have as much right to red or teal as anybody else. I still remember Totie Fields, on the *Tonight Show* years ago, talking about black clothes. She said, "They told me that if I wore this black dress, I would lose fifteen pounds. Right. I put it on, got on the scales, and I didn't lose one damned ounce!"

Totie was right. No matter how great my outfit is, when I get on the scales, I weigh the same (another reason I don't have scales in the house). But this is about optical illusion, remember? I think color blocking is so flattering, and I've used it for so long now with so many different outfits, that it has become a major part of my style statement. Adding vertical lines with color is a personal signature move for me. And along the way, over the years, I've developed a couple of shortcuts and tips that I hope might help you, too, as you experiment with color and line. And in your experiments, never forget the law of the vertical line:

> **Up and down—not round and round.**

It's that simple. You should always look for new ways to add vertical lines. But how? Here are some suggestions:

❖ By choosing the right separates of different colors (like a red blazer over a black turtleneck).

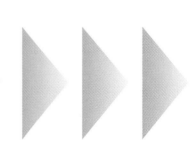

Callie chose a dark green suit, with a gold blouse.

This jacket is a great example of the lines we look for. Maybe you could find one like it in ready-to-wear; then again, maybe not. The inserted side panel is my favorite detail. I love this jacket in a pink, orange, and black version I made for myself.

❖ By adding the right accessories. Long necklaces add a great vertical line; so does a long scarf.

See what a difference a few colorful accessories and a great jacket can make? My son Elliott calls this my Fruit Loop outfit—I can't imagine why.

❖ By using garment embellishment to create a new vertical line (I talk more about this in chapter 12).

❖ By actually introducing the color and line through design and pattern selection. This is true color blocking.

Color Blocking

Color blocking has become very important in the clothes I sew for myself. Let me show you how it's done. Then you can use the principles to buy something similar or to design your own signature pieces.

If you are afraid to put different colors together, buy yourself a new box of crayons and try it out on paper. It's amazing how informative these little crayon pictures can be. It's certainly more economical to eliminate some color choices at the crayon stage, rather than buying fabric and later deciding you don't like the way it looks when you put it together.

The way I use this crayon technique is that I make five or six blank jacket drawings and color them all differently, to see which combination I like best. (You could draw one jacket and make photocopies to play with.) Maybe you're thinking black sleeves, with a red front, and blue shawl collar. Whatever your plan: try it out first with the crayons!

Build up your color courage by experimenting at the crayon stage.

Once you have seen the value of designing with crayons, we can discuss the three specific methods of color blocking.

Method One

Use the pattern as designed. Select a pattern that has strong vertical lines. Even plain solid color garments can provide a good vertical line (for example, a purple turtleneck under a red jacket). However, real color blocking involves cutting

Three different examples of good vertical lines in a jacket pattern.

the pattern pieces out of different colors: like red sleeves on a blue jacket with a white front placket.

Method Two

Modify the pattern pieces. This is when the crayons really come in handy. You can create a yoke where there had been none, or take a plain solid top and draw a diagonal line. Remember my great black dress with diagonal cuts of pink polka dots in chapter 5?

Method Three

This is what happens when you only have scraps of fabric left from other projects. Using the crayons, you can see what a striped fabric might look like and where it might fit into the design of your new outfit. The major difference here is that you are actually building the fabric out of scraps, and then laying down the original pattern piece to cut it out of your newly-built fabric. (This is similar to "Create Your Own Striping," discussed in the Bonus Sewing Section.)

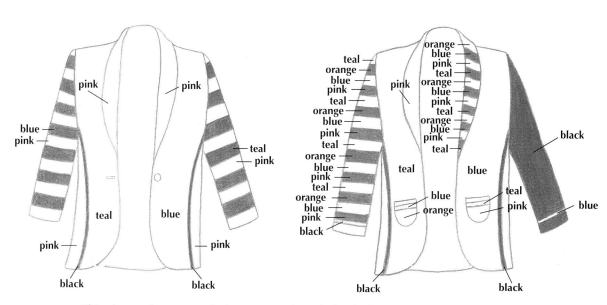

This shows the crayon design. First, I thought both sleeves should be stripes. Then I decided I needed more black, so it evolved.

Taking Off with Color Blocking

Are we having fun yet? I guess I'm hooked.

One thing to think about is establishing a family of colors. Obviously, you'll want to repeat them in various pants, tops, and jackets. By making sure that everything is color-coordinated, you greatly expand your wardrobe. (Here's a case where expansion is a good thing!) Your clothes will be as interchangeable as possible. Then you can wear the same top with two or three different skirts, and the same jackets will work with either your pants, skirts, or dresses. (See chapter 11 for more about building your wardrobe with color.)

The faux piping in the jackets in this section creates a new vertical line. The piping is also used to bring the colors together, and in the first jacket, it is used to blend in one black sleeve. I discuss the faux piping technique in the Bonus Sewing Section—it's easier than you might think!

This wonderful jacket is a combination of color blocking methods. I chose a pattern with good vertical lines, introduced a black faux piping (see the Bonus Sewing Section), and created a striped fabric for the sleeve and one side of the shawl collar. Doesn't Molli Rae look great in it?

(While we're on the subject of jackets: because I often wear longer jackets over knit pants or skirts, Velcro butt can be a common problem. The knit jacket fabric will stick to the knit pant fabric. Definitely not a good thing. But there is a solution to this problem! The jackets shown in this section have the advantage of fusible knit interfacing. By ironing the interfacing on to the fabric before I even cut out the pattern pieces, I have lined the entire jacket in a simple and painless way, and it won't hang up on my very gifted derriere. This is an incredible design technique that will totally eliminate the problem of Velcro butt.)

I have an outfit I love that is like color blocking on Prozac. My original inspiration for this design came to me on a shopping trip in Pittsburgh, when I found

79

Note the layered fringed bottom on the jacket, the bold vertical line created by the teal faux piping, and my trademark car-wash skirt! I call this my Atlantic City Fringe outfit. The techniques are all in the Bonus Sewing Section.

some great shoes, with wonderful geometric designs of hot pink, teal, and royal blue on black leather. The best part—besides the fact that they were a size 10—was that they were 60% off!

For me, color blocking is like reading a Grisham novel. Once you start, you can't stop. And you want to do it again and again. Once I had the shoes, I designed the fringed jacket, knowing it would go with black, teal, pink; with skirts or pants. Those fringes just wanted more, and that's when I made a crayon drawing of my car-wash skirt.

My famous car-wash skirt. Sue Hausmann even wore one on her show, America Sews.

This outfit has it all: strong vertical lines, wonderful color. I finished it off with a splashy necklace and a perfectly matched ultrasuede belt. Those shoes are fabulous. When I wear this outfit, the message I'm sending is "I feel good!" ■

Part Three

PUTTING IT ALL TOGETHER

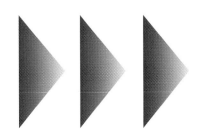

Chapter 11

FABRIC BASICS AND WARDROBE PLANNING

When it comes to clothes, fabric is the basis for everything. (Unless, of course, you happen to be an emperor needing new clothes.) If you think this subject is about as interesting as watching ice melt, skip this chapter. Otherwise, here are some things you might want to know.

Evaluating fabrics

There are a lot of individual factors to consider when choosing a fabric, but they fall into four basic categories.

1. Natural versus Synthetic

Natural fabrics are fabrics made from fibers that come from plants or animals. For instance, silk comes from silkworms; cotton comes from cotton balls; wool comes from sheep. Synthetic fabrics are fabrics manufactured from a thread spun out of a petroleum product, chemical, or a combination. Synthetics include polyester, nylon, acetate, and rayon. Nobody can say cotton is all good or polyester is all bad. It's more complex than that.

The biggest advantage to natural fabrics is that they breathe; they're an excellent choice if you're concerned about the "cool" factor. However, when it comes to cotton fabrics, there are two drawbacks: one is that cotton will shrink; the other is that it will wrinkle.

A wonderful thing about sewing, of course, is that it completely minimizes the shrinkage problem. You launder the raw fabric before you ever cut out the pattern. That gets the shrink out of the way before you make your first scissors cut. (If I were from California, you'd think that was some kind of new-age advice!)

On the other hand, polyester has certainly "come a long way, baby!" The new microfiber polyester looks and feels like real silk. Gorgeous colors. Soft and very drapable.

The best thing about polyester, of course, is that it's wrinkle-free and colorfast. There'll never be any shrink with polyester. Yes, polyester has come a long way since the seventies and that horrible double-knit polyester.

Be careful, though. Double-knit polyester pants are still lurking on some racks of ready-to-wear. Avoid these pants like deviled eggs at an all-day summer picnic. They are hot, bulletproof, and shapeless. If you still own a pair of these, run, don't walk, to the city dump. There is no occasion, no excuse, no reason to put this fabric on your body. Nobody should ever be that depressed. If you're even thinking about it, call a prayer hotline. You can be talked through it.

A most important consideration for me when choosing fabric is whether or not it's washable. (I don't know about you, but I do not have a "Dry Clean Only" lifestyle.) The only way to find out is to look at the care tag on everything you buy. And do exactly what it says. Some natural fabrics are washable: cotton, for instance. But wool is not. The same is true of synthetics. Polyester is very washable, but acetate is not. Each fabric or garment must be considered on its own merits.

As with most things, you get what you pay for. Generally, natural fibers cost more. A dress made out of 100% silk might cost $200, while a garment of microfiber (synthetic) silk might be about $80. A wool sweater might cost $140, whereas an acrylic sweater of similar style might be about $50. The difference in cost is not necessarily because one fiber is superior to the other. It has to do with the cost of production. It's cheaper to spin an acrylic yarn out of a chemical polymer than it is to shear the wool off a sheep, process it, spin it, dye it, etc.

Fortunately, it isn't always an either/or proposition. Sometimes, the best solution can be a compromise. My favorite fabric is 50/50 poly/cotton interlock. This is a knit fabric that is half cotton and half polyester. It's a breathable, cool fabric that is wrinkle-resistant and shrinkproof. I think it's the best of both worlds. Interlock holds its shape, travels well, and almost never needs ironing.

One interlock can be very lightweight, while another one is almost a heavy pant-weight fabric. The difference is not in the fiber content, but in the number of stitches per square inch. Think about buying sheets. The luxury sheets would be 200 threads per square inch. I remember when muslin sheets were 140. They're not widely available anymore, but you can be sure that as the thread count goes up, so does the price of the sheet. It's the same with fabric for ready-to-wear or the sewing industry. You always get what you pay for.

2. Fabric Color

I don't think I can be too emphatic about how important color is to your wardrobe. The color is the first thing people will notice, for good or bad. Color can set the tone, create a mood. Color can lift you up, or bring you down.

Please don't be reluctant to use color. Embrace it. Make it your friend. Find out what colors you look good in. Brights or pastels? Blue or orange? Decisions, decisions. There aren't any right or wrong answers: color is entirely about your own personal taste. Trust your own feelings about color, and once you decide what you like, build your entire closet around your core colors. I'll go into more detail about wardrobe planning at the end of this chapter.

3. Print or Solid?

I think this is an area where we very often make big mistakes. Personally, I seldom wear an outfit that is all-over print. That looks awful on me, for several reasons. First of all, a big, splashy print looks cheap, and just screams "$9.99." The print will also look dated much faster than a solid color would have.

However, I'm not telling you never to wear a print! I have lots of print fabric in my wardrobe, and some of it is pretty flashy. But I usually combine the prints with solids. It can also be very interesting to color block with prints. For instance, I found a wild geometric print that I loved. Instead of doing the con-

Bad idea: the big, splashy print just ends up looking cheap.

ventional thing, I used the wild print for the front and back of a jacket, then chose a polka dot for the sleeves, one white on black, the other black on white. In a perverse way, combining the different prints toned down this jacket! And remember my Fruit Loop outfit, shown in all its glory in Chapter 10? It is a combination of five different print fabrics. I combined solid pink and orange with the various prints, and used the faux piping detail to bring the colors together.

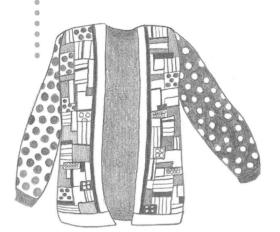

Who would have thought that the answer to toning down this wild geometric print would be to add polka-dot sleeves?

A small-scale print, such as a herringbone tweed or a polka dot, can be an excellent choice to expand your wardrobe. These prints are timeless, and I'm always attracted to fabrics and styles that transcend today and go beyond current trends. (Although you have to wonder about polka dots. My editor, Robbie Fanning, tells me that they are, indeed, named after the very popular dance introduced in Paris around 1843, the polka. So then where are the Tango Dots and Waltz Dots? Hmmmm.)

4. Knit or Woven?

Basically, a woven is just what the name implies. Half the threads are horizontal, and the other half are woven up and down vertically. A knit fabric, on the other hand, is created the same way as knitting a sweater. The thread is looped onto a thousand little curved hooks, and another thread is knit in and out of each loop.

The two finished fabrics are very different. The woven has no stretch (think of a calico fabric), whereas the knit has lots of stretch (think of a T-shirt). The actual amount of stretch in a given knit depends on the type of thread used: if a Lycra thread is introduced, for example, you would have a swimsuit fabric with over 100% stretch.

Knit fabrics will mold and fit easily to body shapes, whereas woven fabrics are more rigid and can be confining. Knit fabrics are more resistant to wrinkling. By the same token, however, knits will not take a sharp crease. Sometimes, knit fabrics can collect surface fuzz, and they have a tendency to snag or grow. For that reason, knit garments should not be hung on hangers but folded, to prevent stretching.

Other Fabric Factors

Even after you've looked at the basic characteristics of a fabric, there are still some other specific factors to consider. For instance, some fabrics have a lovely drape to them. That means they swirl when you twirl. It's the exact opposite of crisp. Usually, the finer the thread used to make the fabric, the more drapable it will be. Here, again, it is not a matter of one kind of fabric being better than the other. It's simply about choosing the best fabric for the pattern or style. For a dressy suit with a blazer and lined skirt, a crisp gabardine or linen would be the best choice. For a long full skirt, however, a drapable, flowing challis or rayon would be best.

There's also that cellulite factor to be considered. I just haven't met the silk that can hold up to my thunder thighs. Although silk is a breathable, natural fabric with beautiful drape, it's too fragile for my required psi (pounds per square inch). Knits, on the other hand, give me some insurance. A little extra give can be a wonderful thing.

Again, all things must be considered. If you fall in love with a fine, lightweight silk fabric, then at least choose a style that is very full: palazzo pants or a full skirt. Then you won't have to worry about the seams ripping or pulling open due to the pressure. Let's face it: we have different pressure points than Kate Moss. I gotta think that if she can cross her legs, and then her ankles, cellulite psi is not something she stays awake worrying about.

Wardrobe Planning

Volumes have been written about wardrobe planning. It's one of those things that means different things to different people, but one aspect just

Kim and Julie are reaping the benefits of keeping a wardrobe to a limited palette of separates that can mix and match!

about every expert agrees on is how important it is to color-coordinate your wardrobe. For example, let's say you look great in red, purple, and black. You can greatly expand your wardrobe by sticking to those three basic colors and making sure everything coordinates.

Take as an example a wardrobe in which you start with three pairs of pants: one red, one purple, and one black. Add three different tops: maybe two in solid colors, and one color-blocked top using all three colors. Already, you can start counting the possible combinations: if two of the tops are turtlenecks and one is a buttondown shirt, you can combine two of the tops for yet another outfit. Then, if you add one vest, one jacket, and one skirt to the collection, the possibilities start to get hard to count! With only nine separate articles of clothing, you will have literally dozens of different outfits available to you.

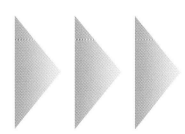

black   red   purple

There may be only nine individual pieces of clothing here, but when you start to count up the ways in which you can combine them…

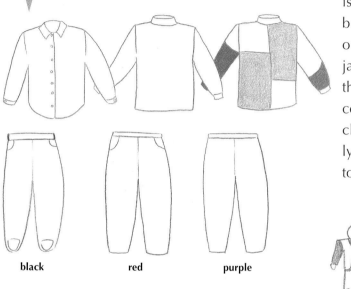

…those nine pieces of clothing add up to dozens and dozens of outfits!

Look at Julie and me in these separates; there's nothing here but red, purple, and black!

You can use the principle of combining matching separates to create a very elegant, professional look, as Beth does here in her red suit.

This is a very simple, basic principle, and one that is not lost on most women. Focusing on three basic colors is a powerful way to expand your wardrobe. You make an even bigger impact when you start to consider belts, scarves, and other accessories. At that point, the possibilities are endless. Think about it. If you opened your closet and every blouse, skirt, jacket, and pair of pants blended and matched, wouldn't it be a snap to put together an outfit? Of course, you have to resist buying that fabulous olive-green pantsuit. No matter how much of a bargain it is, it will only be a headache hanging in your closet.

Using separates to build a wardrobe is a valuable technique for the gifted woman. The fact that many of us do not have run-of-the-mill proportions is another very good reason to choose skirts, tops, pants, jackets, etc., rather than trying to get a dress or one-piece outfit to fit properly. Whether we're talking

Of course, you can also have fun, like Lisa and Brenda, mixing and matching pieces to put together a hip, casual look.

about your working wardrobe or your casual wardrobe, mixing and matching separates is a very effective way to expand your clothing selection.

Wardrobe planning is about deciding what colors look good on you and what you like, and building on that knowledge to create and enhance your own personal style. ▨

Chapter 12

EXPRESSIVE GARMENT EMBELLISHMENT

Are we having fun yet? Now that you're seriously getting into this style thing it's time to explore some of the ways you can express your own personality through the clothes you wear.

Embellishing just means decorating or trimming your garments. Embellishment can be a very creative way to use your imagination to create your own personal, unique style. Done correctly, it is also a great trick, because you get to draw attention to your best features: those you wish to emphasize. Again, it's a way to control the messages your clothes send to the world. I always think of Madonna's song *Express Yourself* when I think of garment embellishment. (Of course, I don't recommend gold-plated breast cones. Some people take things to the limit!)

One of the most exciting things about embellishment is that you don't have to sew the entire garment to create a custom-designed look. You can get great results by decorating ready-to-wear or plain blank garments. Mary Mulari asked me to write a foreword to her book *Garments with Style,* a book I found to be a terrific source of inspiration. Mary walks you through dozens of projects using store-bought sweatshirts, consignment-shop vests, your hus-

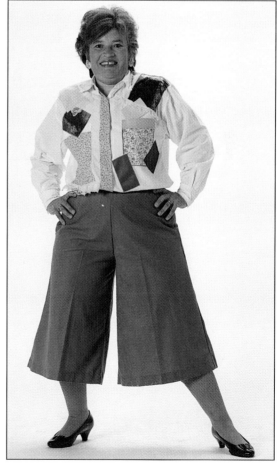

Do you think Ronda could have found this shirt just by walking into a store?

band's old dress shirts, etc. She tells you what to look for when you're shopping, and she writes wonderful directions that will ensure professional results for your garment embellishment. Once you get started, you may not be able to stop!

Mary Mulari, a.k.a. The Appliqué Goddess, is the leading authority in this very hot area of garment embellishment. She has at least ten books to her name at this point. Because she's such a respected teacher and designer in this field, I asked Mary if she had any special advice for those of us decorating gifted-sized garments. She said:

> If a national poll were taken, it would surely reveal that the majority of women are not satisfied with the size and shape of their own bodies. Someone you may see as nearly perfect will surprise you with negative, self-conscious feelings about her ankles or her too-thin upper arms. What makes sense then, for any woman of any size, is to accentuate her best features, drawing the eye away from figure flaws. It is always important to remember that the area we trim is where the viewer's eye is drawn. A flattering place to decorate for most women is the yoke area of a dress or top. Designs around the yoke encircle the garment, and are placed above the bustline and over the top of the shoulders. The effect of a circular yoke design is to frame the face, drawing the viewing eye to a contagious smile and an expressive countenance.

Watch how the circular yoke design on this top draws our eye upwards to the wearer's face.

I think that's great advice from Mary. (Although I'm still trying to picture "too-thin upper arms." This is a problem? Are you kidding? Give me her address and I'll send her a case of Snickers and a carton of extra-butter microwave popcorn.)

Mary goes on to say,

> Decorating clothing with fabrics of the same color as the garment creates a tone-on-tone effect, an understated look of class. It's true that the decoration will not be seen from across a room, but often, this subtle look of texture is preferred. Compare the impact of a large, bold design centered on a shirt with that of a shirt featuring a smaller, graceful decoration placed over one shoulder. Note that the large design accentuates the size of the garment.

To illustrate this point of Mary's, imagine a sweatshirt with a large appliqué design. If the design is centered in the middle of a top, think about where that design will fall on a gifted body: isn't it right over a bulge area?

This is certainly not one of our best areas. For years now, I have been taking Mary's good advice, and placing my embellishments on my yoke area, or on my left shoulder; even around the back of my shirt.

That big design smack dab in the middle of a top is one of the most common mistakes gifted women make. Remember: the area that is embellished is the area people notice. Having a big design in the middle of my top makes me feel like a dining room table wearing a huge centerpiece—generally of the plastic-flower variety.

Garment embellishment is a lot like getting a new perm. When it's done right, it can make you very happy. Everybody will notice and tell you how great you look. Instant style statement. However, if the perm goes wrong, it will definitely do more harm than good.

Mary Mulari points out that this huge design centered right over a woman's bulge area is not the most flattering; it works so much better to put it off-center, up near your face, and enjoy the attention it draws to your smile!

If you are an accomplished sewer, you may already be experimenting with various ways to embellish or decorate your clothes. If you are a novice, or even a virgin sewer, embellishing ready-to-wear clothing can be the perfect place to start.

Try it—you'll like it!! ■

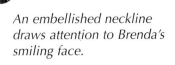

An embellished neckline draws attention to Brenda's smiling face.

Chapter 13
ACCESSORIES WITH ATTITUDE

Accessories should never be neglected. More than anything else, the accessories you choose will establish your own personal style. They polish your outfit and finish your look. They refine your statement and reflect your personality. That's pretty powerful stuff. Your accessories telegraph your message to the world.

Remember the three-second rule.

If you don't believe me, think about it. What do you remember about Bella Abzug? Most of us don't remember her political views, but we all remember those great hats!

There was a character named Melissa on the yuppie television show *thirtysomething*. She always wore just one dangly earring, in her right ear. That accessory made her statement and I found myself looking for it on every show.

I know a teacher who loves scarves. Getting twenty new ones for Christmas every year is an occupational hazard, but the amazing thing is that she can open a drawer full of them, and tell you which one came from which student, what that child's gifts were, what problems he had, etc. Her students look forward to the day when she'll wear the special scarf they gave her to school. In her case, the scarf has gone beyond being an accessory. Her special collection serves as a reminder of all the children who've passed through her classes: a history of her teaching years.

Let's talk for a minute about the basic black dress. I know, I know…I'm always telling you to grab the color wheel, to step back from boring black and be bold, to be yourself. And I mean it. But you've also got to have a basic black dress.

A simple black dress will go with anything. You can dress it up or down. It can go to work or take you out to dinner. It's an essential part of any woman's wardrobe. It's like having iceberg lettuce in the refrigerator—a mealtime basic that can be transformed with just a few additions.

So let's accessorize it. First, we add a versatile two-point scarf with a wonderful reversible purple and black obi belt (look for instructions on how to make both of these in the Bonus Sewing Section). Add some shoes, in the same purple and black as the Obi belt, and some bold, snazzy earrings, and the basic black dress is by now completely transformed. The addition of a few accessories is a powerful way to enhance your look.

Many chapters ago, I talked about where to begin in putting together an outfit, and I told you that often I would start an entire outfit with a great necklace or pair

Deena in the basic black dress. What a difference accessories make: the dress is anything but basic in the photo on the right.

of earrings. This is the "cart-before-the-horse" way of doing things, but a perfect accessory can be the reason you are inspired to put together a fun new look.

There isn't enough paper in this book for me to elaborate on every single accessory option, because the possibilities are endless. But I am going to discuss in depth two major accessory choices that work for me: necklaces and belts. I hope in that way to show you how much joy and style the right accessories can bring into your unique, individual wardrobe.

Necklaces

A loud trashy necklace is often a big part of my personal statement. I have a pegboard in my bedroom to accommodate my collection. I started to buy necklaces as souvenirs. When I put a necklace on—no matter how many years may have passed since I bought it—I am snapped right back to the cute little store in Florida or that wonderful almond farm in California where I bought the necklace to begin with. At some point, I also started receiving necklaces as gifts from friends and family, and now I have quite an extensive collection.

My necklaces have definitely become a signature move for me, and they often set my mood for the day. If you look back at the picture of me in chapter 10 wearing my Fruit Loop outfit, you'll see an orange and pink beaded necklace that's a major part of the whole look. And in that same chapter, there is a picture of me in my Atlantic City Fringe outfit, featuring a big bold thread necklace to go with that ensemble.

Because of my size, big is beautiful when it comes to accessories. For me, it's simply a matter of balance. I like my necklaces long (as well as chunky or gaudy). Something delicate simply gets lost on my body.

A necklace brings the focus up to your face. Your necklace becomes the focal point, and that's where people will look: an excellent way to draw the attention to your great smile and make a little eye contact.

We all have things that must be considered when choosing accessories. For me, my double chins have to be factored in. A choker would be out of the question for me.

Can you even see the little necklace hugging the top woman's neckline? Isn't it more fun and interesting to have a bigger necklace, hanging where people can see it?

It's too tight, and gets lost in the folds of my chin. Very unattractive, not to mention dangerous to my health! Besides, the longer necklace is an optical illusion. It provides a visual line that elongates my neck. Pretty tricky, don't you think?

This short necklace doesn't do anything for this woman's neck. Now look back at the longer necklace. Isn't that a nice long visual line?

I prefer necklaces that are at least thirty inches long, but if I find a great necklace that's too short, I use a necklace extender. Nobody has ever noticed this. Ever. The first one I bought cost me twelve dollars, and it was four inches of links. It was a wonderful invention, but I was always searching for it because I would leave it on the last necklace I wore.

Then my friend Anita (who also suffers from this buy-another-necklace syndrome) gave me a much better idea! Now I permanently loop a piece of rattail onto the end of every necklace to make it the right length. The added advantage of rattail is that it's soft and doesn't rub or pull like the old chain one used to: very important when your necklace weighs five pounds! ("Rattail" is a silk-covered round cord. It comes in dozens of colors and is widely available at craft or fabric stores. Buy a roll of black to start off with.)

Another wonderful variation is to use a strand of elastic thread. This works great! Just loop one end through each end of your necklace, and then tie the ends of elastic together. After that, any necklace can be put on right over your head, and you never have to worry about hooking the clasp. My friend Val has arthritis, so she can't open the lobster-claw clasps that come on most necklaces. Adding elastic thread to all her necklaces has greatly expanded her options when getting dressed in the morning.

This rattail extender gives me the nice, long necklace line I like, and it's soft and doesn't irritate my neck!

Although it's not exactly a necklace, the two-point scarf is one of my favorite accessories (see the Bonus Sewing Section for how to make this scarf). Mostly, I hate scarves. They usually get in the way of my shoulder-length hair and get sticky when I perspire. I also never got any good at learning how to tie them properly. But this simple wonderful scarf is a real exception. You just tie a simple knot, but because of the way it flips, you can get two completely different looks.

Two-point scarves: they're not exactly necklaces, but they serve that same function, giving you color right where it will draw attention to your smiling face.

Belts

As you know, belts are one of my favorite things. Belts, belts, belts! A belt is also the accessory that surprises people the most. For years, belts were a taboo for the gifted woman. We were told never to wear a belt: "they cut you in two." It was the biggest mistake of all: it was—are you ready?—sit down—hold your breath: a horizontal line!

Oh my God! The thing is, if you do this belt thing right, it can add great panache to your style. As you know, I'm a big fan of wearing a long jacket, and when you do that, you only have a four-inch waist (at least as far as anyone can see)!

Yes, she's wearing a horizontal line, but it's only a few inches across!

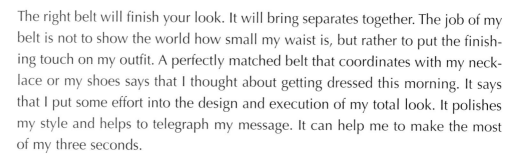

The right belt will finish your look. It will bring separates together. The job of my belt is not to show the world how small my waist is, but rather to put the finishing touch on my outfit. A perfectly matched belt that coordinates with my necklace or my shoes says that I thought about getting dressed this morning. It says that I put some effort into the design and execution of my total look. It polishes my style and helps to telegraph my message. It can help me to make the most of my three seconds.

Not everybody can wear a belt, of course. A good test is to put one on. If the belt rides up, that means you shouldn't be wearing one. Winona can't wear belts, and sometimes even Ruby and Christina are too short-waisted to be comfortable in a belt. If, like my mother-in-law, you feel as though your boobs are the only things that keep the belt from choking you, then you are not a good belt candidate!

I like to think there isn't a fat woman in America who has a better belt collection than I do. And I'm proud. Although I haven't counted them for a long time, they're everywhere. I may have a hundred or so of them, spilling out of suitcases, filling up my dresser, stuffed tight into my drawers, hanging in my closet. (OK: also under my bed, and stuck between the cushions of my sofa. Maybe I've gone over the edge here...)

Women want to know where I find all these great belts. It's a constant search-and-discovery mission. Again, remember my cart-before-the-horse way of doing things. If I find a great belt that fits me, I buy it! Because no matter what color it is, I'll make an outfit to match the belt. Sometimes that's half the fun.

I have to say I often do the reverse, though, too. Sometimes I'll buy or make a wonderful dress but then I can't find the right belt. So in that case, I have to make a belt to match the outfit. You can see I'm very flexible (that is always the key to happiness, girls).

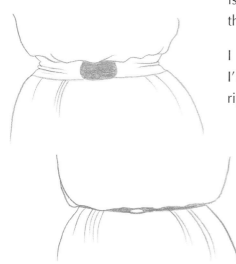

A wide belt gets crushed by fat; a narrow one gets lost in it! Clearly, there has to be another way.

One problem in getting a belt to look good on me is that the sides of the belt often get crushed by the rolls of fat. I tried for about two hours to write that in a more tactful way. Sorry. There's just no other way to describe it. That's what happens. It's a universal problem. Therefore, wide belts are out of the question. However, a narrow little belt looks stupid and also will get lost in the cellulite shuffle. So what's the answer?

I found the answer—the belt that works on a gifted body—in a Lane Bryant store many years ago. It was pink and purple and I didn't have a thing that went with it. But I soon made an outfit to wear with it, and have since bought several others. It's amazing how many things go with pink and purple.

The key to this belt's success is that, although it has a very interesting, big front piece, the rest of the belt gradually narrows to a small rounded elastic band once it gets to the sides of my body. This is the perfect design for me. Again, it has a great focal point in the front (remember your four-inch waist!), yet the sides of the belt are not wide, and don't get crushed or worn down. I love this style!

Of course, nothing is easy for us gifted girls. I've often found a belt like this in a store, only to discover it was that "One Size Fits All." But then I realized that the necklace extender design would also work perfectly to extend

The original belt that solved my belt problems is the final touch that pulls together my fringe outfit.

Here it is: the belt that has a big focal point in the front but narrows along the sides.

a belt! This belt extender idea will work on any belt that has a hook on one end and a loop on the other. What a revelation this was.

Let's say you have a belt that is too small. Take a length of one-inch-wide black elastic (ten inches long or as long as you need it to be) and sew it into a circle. Now poke the elastic circle through the existing loop of the belt, then thread it back through itself and pull tight. That's it! You've just made your belt much bigger. Remember, you're often wearing a long jacket, and most of the time the only part of the belt that is visible is the front four inches! This necklace/belt extender thing is so much fun you won't be able to stop doing it. (For more great belt ideas, look in the Bonus Sewing Section.)

If you're wearing a beautiful jacket, only the front of your belt will show!
Nice finishing touch.

Although I love the look of a chain belt, I could never wear one because the metal they use nowadays just can't hold up to my psi. Cheap metal cannot handle my laugh factor. Most of the time, the links pop under the pressure and little pieces of the belt scatter all over the floor. But: if you add an elastic loop extender, it will be fine.

(The laugh factor gets to be more and more of a consideration as I get older. Who knew that one day laughing would be connected to peeing? It's the stuff your mother never tells you about. Another thing I hate is the chin hair. For crying out loud, I have to carry tweezers in my purse all the time nowadays because that chin hair can grow an inch an hour. When I complained to Mom about it, she said, "Just wait until you're my age. It turns silver, and if you miss it with the tweezers it turns into corkscrewed Christmas tinsel." Gee, I can hardly wait.)

Your Own Signature Accessories

Now you know what my favorite accessories are. So let's get you started. If you think accessories are all about jewelry, think again! Here are some of the possibilities:

- Belts
- Scarves
- Necklaces
- Earrings
- Bracelets
- Pins or brooches
- Shoes
- Purses
- Fingernails
- Rings
- Hats
- Hair ornaments
- Gloves
- Body tattoos (OK, OK, it's all optional, remember)

Accessories can be your best friend. The right accessories make a statement. They can define your look and reflect your personality. You control the messages they send to the world. Your accessories can reflect a certain level of sophistication or they can convey a sense of whimsy and fun.

For example: everybody should have a great basic white oxford blouse. Then, depending on the accessories you choose, you can go western by adding a denim necklace (directions in the Bonus Sewing Section) and a cowboy hat, or you could add a silk scarf and a gold pin for a very elegant look. The accessories completely set the tone. Use your accessories to add finish, panache, and sparkle to each and every outfit you put on. Have a ball! ■

Chapter 14

PERSONAL GROOMING (OR, "ALWAYS WEAR CLEAN UNDERWEAR...")

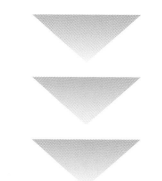

Details: isn't it always the little things that count? Or, at least, it can be the little things that people remember longest. Think about the last time you judged somebody harshly because of a personal hygiene oversight. The examples are everywhere:

❖ The Avon lady comes to your door, and she has really bad breath. Is this the woman you want to buy lipstick from?

❖ A guy asks you out on a date, but you notice his green teeth. Do you decide to give him a chance anyway?

❖ You're shopping for a sewing machine, and the woman who does the demonstration has dirty, cracked fingernails. Do you buy a machine there?

❖ Your child's teacher asks you to come in for a conference, and you have to hang onto a banister to keep from being knocked over by her body odor. Do you leave her office thinking about her great teaching abilities?

❖ Your friend has a job interview, but she's in a hurry and she decides not to wash her hair that day, so it's stringy and greasy. Does she get the job?

I'm sure you get the picture. Situations like this take place every single minute of every single day. We are all judged each and every time we go out in public. Before you know it, your three seconds are up!

We gifted women must deal with stereotyping every single day. America hates fat. It's as if everybody in the country woke up one morning and had been bitten by a Fat Phobia bug. People are terrified of fat. Just walk into a grocery store. Low-fat mayonnaise, for Pete's sake! (I ask you: what would be the point?) My favorite oxymoron is "sugar-free" sugar wafers. Huh?!

We are dealing with a real fat paranoia in this country. Hating fat people is the only acceptable prejudice left in America. All you have to do is look around to know it's true. Have you ever seen an overweight woman doing a hair or make-up commercial? Do they offer us the jobs as front-office receptionists? Are we the television weather girls? According to Diane Sawyer on that *Prime Time* special, we can't even get strangers to help us change a flat tire.

Here's the stereotype: "She's fat, she must be lazy." People assume that to be true. So then it's OK for them to dismiss us. Well, I've got news for America. I might be fat, but nobody I know gets more work done in a day than I do! I have a high-energy life, and I accomplish as much in a 24-hour day as any skinny woman in America.

Being fat is apparently a bad, bad thing. The front cover of the January l994 issue of *People* magazine had pictures of Hollywood celebrities with the headline: "Diet Winners and Sinners." What? Sinners? What's the message here? If you can't lose weight then you must be evil? Puh-leeze!

So what can we do about it?

The thing is, we cannot change society's view of us. That would be unrealistic, like wishing for doctors to lower their fees, or politicians to be honest. A perfect waste of our valuable time. Forget about it! You can never change other people. You can only change yourself. Just remember that: you can only change yourself.

What we have to concentrate on is not reinforcing negative stereotypes.

That's what's so important about the personal grooming. The truth is, if a woman has put on some weight, she probably isn't feeling great about herself. So we have that "low-self-esteem" thing going on.

Here's what starts to happen: I feel awful about the way I look. I look in a mirror and get depressed. I don't even want to go out. I refuse to buy clothes for the size I am right now. I hate my body. Why bother getting a haircut or buying new underwear? There's no point in doing my fingernails today; nobody will see them anyway. Who cares if my nylon knee-highs have five runs in them? What's the point of washing my hair or shaving my legs?

Pretty soon, I'm feeling so depressed, I don't even want to get out of bed in the morning! It's that powerful negative snowball again bowling me over. It's more than a snowball, actually. It's more like a blizzard. And wherever we go, we carry along our own little snow-making equipment.

Been there? Done that? Can you see how the negative feeds on the negative? We buy into the perception that if we are overweight, we are worthless. Pretty soon, you won't know whether you don't have any clothes that fit because you never go out, or you never go out because you don't have any clothes that fit!

Either way, you are the loser: bigtime! It is a mind game.

We do it to ourselves. Really. We reinforce those negative stereotypes. We are our own worst enemy. We actually think so little of ourselves that we refuse to buy decent clothes that fit. We are seen in public in tight, ill-fitting, pull-on polyester pants. Our hair is greasy, and we haven't showered in days. If we have such a low opinion of ourselves, how can we expect the people we meet to respect us?

That's what's so important about personal grooming habits. These are the little daily things that show our self-respect. Really.

If we value ourselves, then the world will, too.

Be meticulous about yourself. You will not only feel much better each and every day you get out of bed, but you'll make a better first impression.

I've been on both ends of this. Because I've suffered from extreme low self-esteem, I've been casual about certain areas of my own personal grooming habits. And also, because I dealt with the public every day, I have often encountered other women who failed to take proper care of themselves. That's when I realized how lasting a negative first impression can be! This might seem like small stuff, but it all comes together to make a big statement.

Pay Attention to the Details

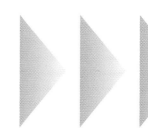

Make this feel-good regimen a regular part of your life:

Shower Daily

You should always smell fresh and soapy. Lots of women came into my store who didn't. (And incidentally, many of them were quite thin!) Let me tell you that body odor makes a very lasting negative impression! We'd talk about them for days.

Pamper Your Hair

Go beyond keeping your hair clean and shiny. Spoil yourself with a wonderful haircut or a new perm. Experiment with the great new hair colors on the market. Find a hairdresser who is fabulous and treat yourself. Often, a woman's hair can be her best and most noticeable feature.

Notice Your Nails

Look at your nails right now. Are they clean? Manicured? Polished? It is amazing how many women don't pay attention to this important detail. Especially when you consider that almost everybody you meet will notice them. You can't shake their hand, drink a cup of coffee or pick your nose without somebody getting a good look at your fingernails. Be aware. Take a little time.

Shave Regularly and Often

When I was pregnant with Elliott, I had gotten very lazy about this grooming detail. When my contractions were two minutes apart, I couldn't go to the hospital until I had shaved under my arms (it was so bad, I feared the nurses would be making jokes about braiding my armpits!). He was born eleven minutes after we arrived at the hospital: too close for comfort, to be sure.

Learn About Makeup

I wear very little makeup, but I do have some basic skills when it comes to foundation, powder, and lipstick. I look and feel better when I've taken the time to apply them correctly. We have all experienced watching a woman walk into the room who made a great first impression because she had on the perfect makeup. You can do that, too: there are many people out there who are eager to teach you everything you ever wanted to know about makeup! So go for it.

Be Vigilant about Your Breath

This goes beyond brushing your teeth in the morning and at night. Carry a small toothbrush with toothpaste in your purse. Brush before an important meeting. After every lunch.

Nothing boosts my confidence like a clean, fresh smile. You'll feel it and so will the people you meet. I don't think anything makes a quicker negative impression than bad breath. It just knocks you over, doesn't it? We've all been on the receiving end, and it's offensive. So be careful! Don't ever forget that a great smile can be your very best asset! It can make a very positive and lasting first impression.

Buy Wonderful Underwear

I'm serious. Maybe nobody else will know you're wearing great-looking underwear...but you will. (Hey, maybe you'll get lucky and somebody actually will notice!) It will make a difference in the way you carry and handle yourself. It took me years to get to this point, but now I can spend over twenty-five dollars on a bra and feel good about it. Having a bra that actually fits correctly can make an amazing difference in the way your clothes look on your body, as well. Give this a try and see if I'm right.

Wearing beautiful underwear puts a different spin on the day. Remember: your mother always told you to wear clean underwear because you never knew when you might be in an accident. This goes way beyond that! Who knows? You might want to date the ambulance driver!

Check those Nylons

OK, OK, so this is something we often forget. It's easy to be caught with a run in our nylons, so why not put them on anyway, and act surprised if somebody notices? I could get an academy award for this one: "Oh no! A run! It must have just happened!"

Yeah, right. This is a small detail, I know. But if somebody notices a run in my nylons, it is one more negative thing to reinforce their already negative stereotype. Don't make it easy for them. Be meticulous.

Remember Your Posture

Posture is so important. Remember that our carriage is the first thing people notice that we can actually control. It says everything about us.

Remember the woman who shuffles into the room with rounded shoulders, looking down at the ground? This alone makes a certain statement about how she feels about herself. She is sending messages to all the people she meets. What is she saying?

Remember this woman? She wants to disappear, but she isn't succeeding.

109

This woman, on the other hand, has no intention of disappearing. She makes a great first impression because she carries herself so well.

And remember the other woman, who walks confidently into the room, with her head held high, her shoulders straight and square, and a smile on her face? She looks directly into the eyes of the person she is meeting, and chances are she has already made a good first impression because she exudes presence.

Why Grooming Is So Important

A very big part of this battle is how we feel about ourselves.

A new haircut, a manicure, some makeup: maybe these things seem trivial. But put together, they make up the message we are sending to the world. This is how we show how much we value ourselves. The time and energy you put into your personal grooming will come back to you many, many times.

Let's review. When you're having the perfect day, and everything is coming together, and you feel on top of every situation: didn't you start the day with a shower and a shampoo? Didn't you take some care when choosing your clothes? Don't they feel just right? Didn't you spend some extra time on your makeup?

The big question is: how are these things connected? That's the mystery. Do other people treat us better because we took the extra time to be meticulous about our grooming on that day? Or could it be that we project a more poised, confident image because we feel that much better about ourselves, knowing all the details have been carefully attended to?

For me, it's a lot like a microwave oven: I don't need to know why it works, only that it does! I know that if I take the time to do these things for myself, it's like buying insurance for a good day.

And hey: a girl can never have too many of those! ■

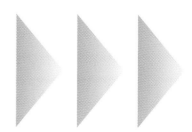

Conclusion

LIFE IS MAKING CHOICES

Each morning when Ross and Elliott get out of bed, I tell them they have only two choices. We all do. It doesn't matter who you are: Michael Jordan, Princess Diana, or President of the United States. You have only two choices:

1. You can decide to be happy and have the best day possible, making the most out of what God gave you.

2. You can be miserable, and pretty much suck the joy out of the day for yourself and everybody around you.

Abraham Lincoln said: "It is my observation that most people are just about as happy as they make up their mind to be."

It's true. It doesn't matter if you are rich or poor, fat or thin, man or woman, married or single: being happy is a personal choice. I always tell my audiences that joy is a gift you give yourself.

You are worth it. I've tried to say that in a hundred different ways, but nothing will change in your life until you believe it. You are worth it. No matter what you weigh, you deserve to be happy. And you can be, despite the weight. But you have to separate those two things. Being happy does not depend upon being thin. If you were thinner, would you be a better wife? A more loving mother? A more caring sister or compassionate friend?

Oprah Winfrey doesn't have a more loyal fan than me. (I wanted to say I was her biggest fan, but then it becomes a weight thing again.) I loved her when she was fat and I loved her thin. Then I loved her again fat. Now I love her again thin. Although I feel as though I suffered through every weight problem and national tabloid headline with her, what she weighed never mattered to me.

Conclusion

Because I knew what was in Oprah's heart. And that was the important stuff, not her size. Not to me. But it was always an issue for Oprah. It seemed sad to me that she could not be happy until she lost the weight.

I have been completely "Oprahtized." But on the issue of weight, we just have to agree to disagree. She's done dozens of shows dealing with the fat issue. And it's not just her. This topic has been on every talk show in America. The consensus by the talk-show experts is that the weight is a symptom of a deeper, more complicated, serious, buried, unresolved "issue."

Those talk-show "experts" say we use the fat as an excuse. That we hide behind it. Like "I'm so fat, nobody will hire me: so why even apply?" Or "I'm so fat, no guy would even look at me, so why worry about having a relationship?" Get it? We supposedly use our fat as a Get Out of Jail Free card. We use it as a shield to protect us from getting bumped around on the Monopoly board of life.

Wow. Do you think that could be true?

Could be. I certainly don't pretend to know. But isn't there just the slightest possibility that there aren't any complicated subliminal psychological motivations here? Couldn't it be a simple, everyday, ordinary, common, been-around-forever difference: some people are thin and some people are not?

I've decided that for now, just for right now, I will accept my large, imperfect body. Maybe one day I'll get the "click" in my brain that Oprah got. And I still do dream about losing a hundred pounds. But in the meantime, I'm going to quit punishing myself. My new mission is to enjoy each and every moment.

We all remember those dramatic "first" moments: our first real kiss. The first time we made love, and the first time we didn't want to. Our first day on a real job. Our first airplane ride. But how about the "last" moments? They, too, are turning points in our lives. But, sadly, they usually go unnoticed and unheralded. They escape us because we never know when they're coming.

When Elliott was a toddler, he'd fall asleep in odd places, and I'd have to carry him up to his room. That doesn't seem possible now. Why don't I remember that last trip up the stairs with him in my arms?

When Ross was small, he loved to pick dandelions. When was the last time he brought me a big bouquet of bright yellow dandelions? I had no idea it would never happen again.

I wish I had known. I wish I had relished those moments.

Sooner or later, you will lose a loved one. Then, you will remember with clarity the last time you kissed them good-bye. Or ate a meal with them. Or laughed with them. The sad thing is, by the time you realize it was an important moment, it's too late to do anything about it. That's the problem. Moments are very fragile things. We're often so busy worrying about what we weigh and what size clothes we wear, we miss the moments.

I spend a lot of time in airports. One day, there was a young man in a uniform getting on the same flight as me. His whole family was there to say a tearful good-bye. I watched those parents with a real understanding of how difficult and significant that moment was. I tried to imagine sending my son off to the military. Where would he sleep that night? Would he be safe? When would I see him again? I knew that family would remember that moment for the rest of their lives. What they were wearing, what they said to each other. Smiles and glances that were exchanged. Hugs shared, tears shed. Of course they would remember. It was an important moment.

I watched that family, and I remember thinking that each moment should be that important. We let life get away from us. We should live with more intensity.

It goes beyond getting up in the morning and deciding to be happy. We should be passionate and enthusiastic about the people we love and the things that we do. That's how you make your life matter. Please don't let your fixation with your weight suck the joy out of your life. Because it can happen. I know. I've been there. I've done that.

Does this make any sense at all? Please don't waste another moment. When you wake up tomorrow, choose to have a good day. You deserve to be happy, no matter what you weigh. You have everything you need to succeed, inside of you, right now. Joy can only come from inside. When you get up, make a plan. Put a smile on your face, a spring in your step, and wear the best outfit you can put together. Face the day with eagerness and attitude. Be sure there's something more important in your life than what you weigh.

Wear clothes that are stylish and attractive: something that fits you right this minute.

It will make a difference. You will feel good about yourself.

Anticipate a great day. Be kind to the kid bagging your groceries. Visit an aunt in a nursing home. Sing along with the car radio. Meet an old friend for lunch. Give three sincere compliments. Smile at the people you meet, knowing they will smile back. Remember, you have everything you need to succeed.

Conclusion

I think about my moments now. I try to make the most of them, recognize and treasure them. Because when I began to assess the things in my life that are truly important, my weight and my size were not even on the list. My worth cannot be measured by the bathroom scales. It can only be measured by real and true relationships.

Well, then, why all this talk about developing a personal style? Why does it matter?

Because: that's the secret, don't you see? It's just like raising kids. The reality, the truth, the thing you must never forget, is that children have an amazing ability to live up to or down to an adult's expectation. Every time. Without fail.

And that's just it, girlfriend. Our style, our clothes, the way we carry ourselves: that's the thing we must live up to. Or down to.

You already are the best of the best. Believe that. Value yourself, and put forth the best exterior possible. Then you will be free to concentrate on the important stuff, the inside stuff.

Do the things you are most scared to do. All of them. Go back to school. Travel. Teach. Write a book. Refuse to be defined by your weight or your size. Marvel at and enjoy the adventure that is your life. Because your life is not about how much you weigh or what size dress you wear.

Yes, right now, at this moment, I am fat. But that's not all I am. My life is about much more than that. And so is yours. ▪

Appendix

BONUS SEWING SECTION

This book is not about sewing. This book is about how difficult it is to live life in the fat lane of a country that worships thinness. This book is about developing a personal style. I hope it's about learning to value yourself, not for what you weigh, but for who you are.

That said, I have to tell you that for me personally, sewing has always been part of the solution to the clothes/style/fit problem of being a gifted woman. But maybe you don't sew well. Maybe you don't sew at all. Perhaps you'd rather tune a piano, clean the oven, spend a week with your mother-in-law or count the raisins in a box of Raisin Bran. You can skip this entire section of the book. However, I think there are some compelling reasons to at least consider sewing:

❖ Sewing makes you the designer. You get to control it all. You get to choose the perfect color, fabric, and style!

❖ Sewing is a creative hobby that can provide great personal satisfaction, hours of enjoyment, and clothes that truly fit and reflect your personality.

❖ And let me get specific: one of the biggest advantages of sewing your own clothes is that you get the opportunity to pre-shrink your fabric. It is wonderful to be able to wash and dry the fabric before the pattern is cut. Have you ever had a brand new pair of pants shrink after washing them the first time? I rest my case. We gifted women have enough fitting problems in the world without that.

Here's my point, girlfriend: you can sew if you want to! Sewing has drastically changed, even just in the last ten years. Like so many other things, it has come a long way, baby.

Think about computers. Twenty years ago, computers were big and awkward, with instruction books six inches thick. Today we have Windows, and even I can do it! The same is true of today's sewing machines. Many of them have jam-proof features, they automatically select the right stitch, and they do a perfect buttonhole at the touch of a button. And today's sewing patterns are based on easy, simple, improved techniques. The instructions don't look like a space shuttle launch anymore.

The patterns I use are "my kind of patterns." They are simple and easy to understand. Look: if you're an advanced sewer, you don't need any encouragement from me. If you consider yourself advanced: Bravo! However, if you are a novice sewer (or even a virgin), then I want to assure you that you, too, can design and sew your own clothes. There is a new age dawning. I hope you'll want to try. You might surprise yourself.

Let's jump right into the easiest things you can sew.

Easy Accessories

Rita's Ruana

This is a wonderful, versatile topper that can be a no-sew project. But it still requires your stepping into a fabric store, and that's a beginning. A ruana is an especially good choice for the gifted woman because of the "no fit" aspect of it.

1 You need 2 yards of 60-inch-wide knit fabric. I recommend a poly/cotton double-knit. Open the fabric to the full 60-inch width. Then fold the fab-

The Ruana is a versatile accessory. Make it up in wool for a great winter coat that fits perfectly. Or try elegant silk for an evening out. Here Mollie Rae shows off a kicky blue Ruana.

ric in half the other way, so that the 60-inch sides meet. Mark this halfway line. It is the shoulder line of your Ruana.

2. The front slit of the Ruana is created by cutting along the natural foldline of the knit fabric (which is 30 inches from each edge) up to the shoulder line. Now round the edges that will create the neckline of the Ruana. You could also round the six corners of the Ruana if you like.

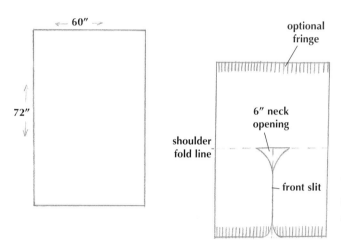

Take a 60-inch by 72-inch piece of fabric. First cut the front slit. Then round the neckline edges and—if you like—the corners. Voilà! A Ruana.

3. The edges can be left raw if you're using a nonfray fabric, such as Polar Fleece. They can also be cut into fringes, hemmed, or trimmed with an overcasting decorative thread in your serger (for more information on sergers, see page 123).

Wear it like a cape, or throw one side up over your shoulder. A Ruana is truly one size fits all. It's also an excellent choice for evening wear. Think velvet…

Flip the ruana over one shoulder for a sophisticated look.

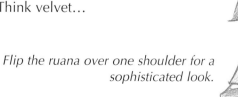

The denim necklace creates a casual yet distinctive look. It can even "go Western" with the right hat and skirt.

Denim Necklace

Here's another great no-sew project.

1. First, simply cut off the waistband section of a worn-out pair of blue jeans. That's right: just take a pair of scissors and cut through the pockets and everything else, about 2 inches below the waistband.

Cut out the waistband plus 2 inches from a worn-out pair of jeans.

2. Cut away the pocket fabric behind the denim, trimming closely with your scissors.

3. To create the fringe, cut into the denim from the raw edge up to the waistband every $1/2$-inch all the way around your piece. You're done!

4. Don't forget this very important step, though: launder your necklace repeatedly. As you wash it, a wonderful "blooming" will start to occur. Wash and dry it at least three times.

Wear the denim necklace plain or lace a colorful bandanna, a man's necktie, or a coordinating strip of fabric in the belt loops. The bigger the jeans, the longer the finished necklace.

Two-Point Scarf

A half yard of 45-inch-wide fabric will make one two-point scarf. Challis is a good choice for the fabric, but any soft polyester or silk will result in a smashing accent for your wardrobe.

1. Copy the two-point scarf pattern piece, using the dimensions shown (in inches), onto a piece of paper large enough to fit the 21-inch side. (After you have drawn the three straight edges, use one flowing motion, curving from your elbow, to draw the curve.)

The two-point scarf lies flat and looks great without ever getting in your way.

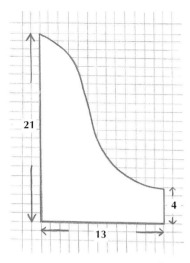

21

4

13

Two-point scarf pattern: the numbers shown are dimensions in inches.

2. Cut the pattern piece out of fabric four times. Cutting curves can be challenging, so do your best with the curve.

3. Sew two of the pieces, right sides together, at the 4-inch edge, as shown. Repeat with the other two pieces. Now you should have two "scarves," each looking like the letter Z.

seam

When you sew two pattern pieces together at the 4-inch edge, you get a large letter Z.

4. Lay the two Z-shaped half-scarves on top of each other, right sides together. Pin. Using a $1/4$-inch seam, sew first the straight edges and then the curve from point A around to point B. Finally, sew the curve from point C around to point D, leaving a 2-inch opening to turn.

5. Turn your scarf right side out, whip stitch the opening, and press.

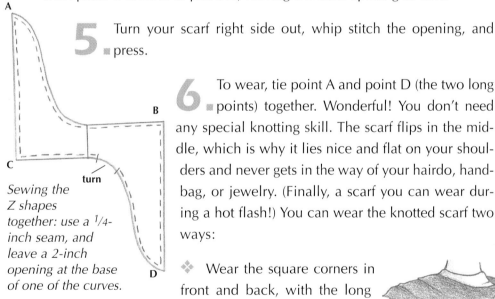

A

B

C

turn

D

Sewing the Z shapes together: use a $1/4$-inch seam, and leave a 2-inch opening at the base of one of the curves.

6. To wear, tie point A and point D (the two long points) together. Wonderful! You don't need any special knotting skill. The scarf flips in the middle, which is why it lies nice and flat on your shoulders and never gets in the way of your hairdo, handbag, or jewelry. (Finally, a scarf you can wear during a hot flash!) You can wear the knotted scarf two ways:

❖ Wear the square corners in front and back, with the long points knotted on your shoulder.

❖ Or, wear with the square corners on your shoulders and the knot in center front, for that sailor collar look.

This scarf makes an elegant gift, too. Good luck!

Tube Belt

This is a very easy belt to make. And the best part about it is you don't have to measure your waist.

1. Wrap a length of 1¼-inch sport elastic around your waist until it is snug, but comfortable. It's going to be a belt, remember. Add 1 inch at each end, then cut the elastic.

2. Now, measure and cut your fabric. The width of the fabric piece will be 3 inches. To determine the length of the fabric, add 15 inches to the length of the elastic. (For example, if my belt elastic is 32 inches long, my piece of fabric is going to 47 inches long.) You add the extra inches because the elastic stretches, but the fabric doesn't.

3. To sew the fabric "tube," fold the fabric in half lengthwise, right sides together, and sew the long seam with a ¼-inch seam allowance.

4. Turn the tube of fabric right side out, and press it. Now insert the elastic. Attaching a safety pin to the elastic or using a bodkin will help you nudge the elastic through the tube.

5. Position the seam of the fabric along the center back of the belt. Sew along that seam line, stretching the belt as you

Stitch along the back seam line to finish the belt.

sew. Be sure to use matching thread; this stitching will show. Another great design detail, common on Liz Claiborne designs, is accomplished by stitching along the top and bottom edges of the elastic, remembering to stretch the belt as you sew.

6. Attach plain belt closures from a fabric store to each end. Loop the ends of the belt through the hardware and fold the last ½ inch of each end to the back of the belt. Stitch the ends down to hold the closure hardware in place.

7. These simple belt closures are boring, so when I put the belt on, I normally wear them in back. Then I attach a more interesting brooch, buckle, or appliqué piece to match my outfit for the front of the belt. Remember, because I'm often wearing a long jacket, people only see the center front four inches of my belt!

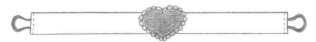

Instead of letting the boring belt closures show, I use those key front four inches to show off an interesting decoration.

Belt Extensions

Elastic Loop Extension

I talked about this loop extension in chapter 13, but it's so great, I want to remind you about it here. If your belt has a hook on the back, as many do, this is the answer.

Elastic loop extension: it's amazingly simple and nobody sees it.

Using 1-inch-wide black elastic, cut a piece 10 inches long (or longer or shorter, depending on your needs). Thread the piece of elastic through the existing loop on the belt and sew the elastic ends together.

That's it! Wow! Talk about easy. I've been known on occasion to make an emergency extension by attaching a safety pin to the elastic. Remember, I'm usually wearing a jacket, so nobody sees the back of my belt anyway!

Elastic Belt Extender Insert

This method works on those dressy belts that you find in retail, made out of things like satin fabric. A belt like this often has fancy sequins or a bejeweled front piece. It can be the perfect accessory for that great pair of black palazzo pants. Just what you need for the office Christmas party. That's the good news. The bad news is they never, never come in large sizes. But you can buy that belt, even if it's "One Size Fits All," and make it work, with a simple adjustment.

1. Cut off a 2-inch piece at each end of the belt you've bought, and hang onto the pieces (you'll sew them back on in a minute).

2. Cut two pieces of elastic (black elastic will be fancier), each the same length (let's say 3 inches long). Now insert the elastic: sew one of these elastic pieces to each end of your belt, and then sew the 2-inch belt pieces back on to the elastic ends. (You might want to cover the elastic with a matching fabric before sewing it in, but if you're lucky, your black elastic matches the satin just fine.)

3. After you've reattached the original closure ends, the belt is 6 inches (or as much as you like) longer, and nobody is the wiser!

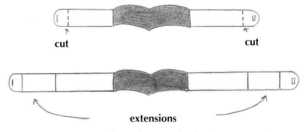

No one ever needs to know the belt wasn't always this long!

One sleeve and one lapel of this jacket are "striped." Also, note the black faux piping inserted in the seam under the sleeve.

Optical Illusions and Decorative Decoys

Create Your Own Striping

The color-blocked striped-sleeve jacket we discussed in chapter 10 uses this striped fabric on the sleeve and lapel. You might want to use only two colors, or six colors, or random colors, but for the purpose of these instructions, I'll work with three different colors (A, B, and C).

Begin with 1 yard of each color to yield 3 yards of striped fabric.

1. Cut each yard of fabric into 3-inch strips (or 2-inch strips or 4-inch strips, depending on how wide you like your stripes). Be sure to cut crossgrain. (Cutting crossgrain will be especially important if the fabric is a knit, in which case the strips will be very stretchy.) The easiest way to cut all the strips is to fold the fabric in half and use a rotary cutter with a good long straight edge.

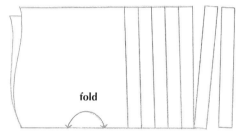

Fold your fabric in half and cut crossgrain strips, as wide as you like your stripes.

TIP

Just a note about the crossgrain. Knit fabrics are usually sold in 60-inch widths, and they usually have a fold at the 30-inch lengthwise center. The straight of the grain runs parallel to that fold line. Therefore, the crossgrain, as shown above, is perpendicular to the fold line. Cutting on the crossgrain gives you consistent 60-inch-long strips that have the most stretch possible.

2. Sew strips together in sets of three: with right sides together, sew each A strip to a B strip, then each B strip to a C strip. You should now have 12 three-color sets (18, if you're using 2-inch stripes).

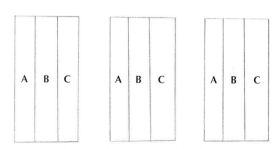

Your three-color strips will look like this.

3. Now sew your sets together by joining each A to the C of the set next to it. When you get this done, you

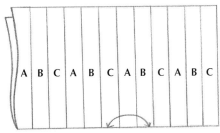

Your finished fabric has the repeating pattern you create by sewing the sets together.

will have 2$\frac{1}{2}$ yards of finished striped fabric (you lose the rest to seam allowances).

4. This new striped fabric you've made can be used the way you would use any other fabric. Place your pattern pieces and cut. You can make one striped sleeve, like I did. Or maybe use stripes for just the left front of your jacket. It's up to you.

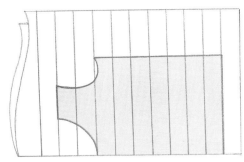

You can lay pattern pieces on this striped fabric and cut, just as you would with any other fabric.

THE SERGER ADVANTAGE

If you are working with a knit fabric, like my favorite 50/50 interlock, I strongly recommend using a serger. If the knit is very stretchy, use the differential feed. Test sew on scraps of the fabric, and if it comes out too rippled, set the differential on 2.0.

If you don't know what a serger is, please go into your nearest sewing machine shop and ask for a demonstration. A serger is not a sewing machine. It does three things at once: seams, cuts, and overcasts the edges with thread. Sergers have been used to manufacture clothing for many years, but in the last decade, this little dynamo has revolutionized the home sewing industry.

TIP

Don't throw away even the smallest scrap of this beautiful fabric. Sue Hausmann featured a garment on her show, *The Art of Sewing,* using striped fabric for ribbing. It was a knockout.

Keep those striped scraps to use for strategic impact.

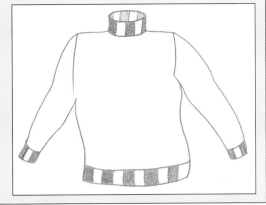

A N O T H E R   T I P

The first outfit I made using this technique started with a "real" striped fabric, a white and turquoise knit with $1/2$-inch stripes. I loved the colors, but did not want the stripes going around my hips. So I bought a yard each of white and turquoise, cut 4-inch strips, and built enough fabric for the skirt. It was a smashing dress. I only wish I could still fit into it...

By building the fabric myself for the skirt of this dress, I could make the stripes go my way!

Faux Piping

OK, this isn't really piping. It's simply a folded strip of knit fabric inserted between two pattern pieces. And it has no stuffing, as regular piping would. But faux piping is an effective, striking design detail.

Faux piping is a wonderful way to introduce a new color, or tie other colors together. For the purpose of explaining this technique, we'll use it in a simple six-gore skirt. Imagine a black skirt with red piping between each gore. Or maybe the skirt is red and purple with black piping. Pretty sharp, eh?

Faux piping creates a great vertical line on the front of my Fruit Loop jacket.

1. The piping itself is simply a strip of interlock fabric, cut crossgrain. Use a rotary cutter with a good long straight edge to cut the strips. These strips will be very stretchy, which is important when you're inserting them in curves. (For this example, we'll cut the strips 2 inches wide, and the visible finished faux piping will be $1/2$-inch wide.)

2. To create the piping, fold the 2-inch strip lengthwise, down the middle, wrong sides together and right sides out.

Fold your piping strip lengthwise before you insert it between the pattern pieces.

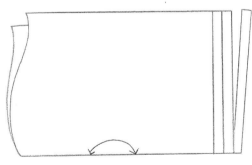

Make sure you cut your piping strips crossgrain in the stretchy interlock fabric.

3. Insert the piping between two skirt pieces as you seam them together. Use your fingers to hold things together. (You might want to pin ahead every ten inches or so, to keep the two skirt edges and two piping edges straight.)

4. Knit fabric is usually 60 inches wide, which means your strips of piping will be very long. There's no need to precut the piping to fit the pattern piece. Simply lay the piping between the pattern pieces and sew (or serge) without stretching it. Then, cut off the excess piping when you get to the end of the seam.

Don't worry about the length of the piping; just cut off the excess at the end of the seam.

TIP

Again, it's best to work in sets. Sew just one set together at a time (each set consisting of two pattern pieces plus piping). This technique helps to keep things straight and on-grain, and it's easy to end up with a parallelogram.

It's easier to keep everything under control if you sew the piping and pattern pieces together in sets before putting it all

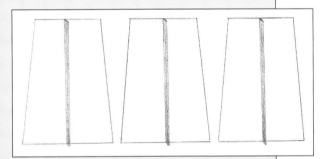

ANOTHER TIP

I've worked with strips from 1 to 3 inches wide. If you want a wide piping, insert according to the directions above, then steam the finished piping down to one side (be consistent) and topstitch with your regular sewing machine. Use a stretch needle. This wider piping is very effective, and looks like a complicated inserted stripe.

Faux piping is a fantastic design detail. It can introduce a contrasting color or bring the existing colors together, all the time adding that important vertical line. It's wonderful in a gored skirt, in the princess seam of jackets and/or dresses, along the top of a sleeve, down the outside of pants, in the yoke of a top or blouse. Try it, you'll like it!

Layered fringe gave flair to the jacket of my Atlantic City Fringe outfit.

Layered Fringe

The layered fringe technique is easier than hemming. It looks wonderful at the bottom of a jacket or duster, top, skirt, dress, or vest. Take your pick.

This technique works with most knit fabrics, but test a sample first. Interlock won't ravel or roll, whereas a lighter weight single knit will roll into itself, which is also an interesting look. For this example, we'll add fringe to the bottom of a jacket.

The layered fringe jazzes up the bottom of this duster, and it's easier than hemming.

1. Cut out your jacket pattern pieces as usual.

2. Construct the jacket but don't hem it.

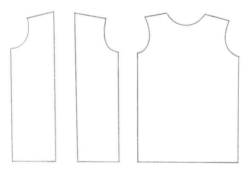

Make your jacket, cutting and sewing as usual, but don't hem it.

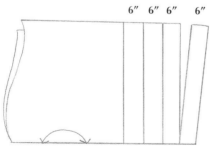

6" 6" 6" 6"

For a 6-inch-long fringe, I cut 6-inch-wide strips from each piece of fabric.

3. Let's say this jacket is black, and the fringe is going to be blue, pink, and teal. I take three pieces of interlock fabric, one in each of those colors, and I want the fringe to be 6 inches long, so I cut 6-inch-wide crossgrain strips out of each piece of fabric.

4. Taking one piece, 60 inches long by 6 inches wide, from each of the three fabrics, make

blue
pink
teal

6″

The three strips, one of each color, are basted together in a sandwich.

a sandwich of the three pieces. Machine baste (or use a serger) across the top of the sandwich, sewing through all three layers.

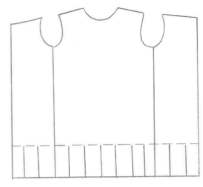

5. Pin your three-color sandwich to the inside of the bottom of the jacket, making sure the edges are even. From the inside of the jacket, stitch through all layers, along the top of the sandwich.

6. Now, with scissors, cut the three-layered sandwich you've sewn to the inside of the jacket into fringes. You can make your cuts half an inch or 1 inch apart, or however wide you want your fringes to be.

Here is your fringed jacket. The dotted line shows the stitching that attaches the three-colored layer to the jacket; the vertical lines are the fringe cuts.

TIP

You can make this fringe out of little pieces of leftover fabric. If you have only small pieces of one of the colors, butt them up against each other when you're building the sandwich. Once you cut the fringes, it won't matter!

Car-Wash Skirt

2½″

hip line

3½″

36″

5½″

The car-wash skirt pattern piece: this is the only one you'll need, and you use it over and over to make the skirt as wide as you like.

The car-wash skirt is another fun, fringed piece of clothing. Amazingly, it uses just one simple pattern piece.

I cut plenty of panels for my car-wash skirt, because I wanted it full.

1. First determine how many pattern pieces you need. Take your hip measurement. Let's say that measurement is 48 inches (don't I wish). The pattern piece is 3½ inches (3 inches finished) at the hip line, so you need 16 pieces (48 divided by 3) just to fit around your body. Allow at least 2 or 3 extra panels for ease. If you want the skirt full, you can add up to 8 more panels for extra flip and flare (my car-wash skirt has 24 panels in it).

2. The other piece of math you have to do has to do with the number of colors in your skirt. It's just this: make sure the number of panels can be divided by the number of colors you want in the skirt. With three colors, for instance, make sure the number of panels can be divided by 3 (18, 21, 24, or 27 panels would work). You need to do this math to make sure a color will never have to touch itself in the finished skirt, and the repeating pattern of colors can continue unbroken around the whole skirt.

3. Choose a number of panels that satisfies the math requirements in both step 1 and step 2. For the skirt I'm showing you here, we'll use 18 panels (remember: for our example we needed at least 16 to fit the hips, and it had to be divisible by 3 because we're using 3 colors). This means we'll cut out 6 red, 6 purple, and 6 black pattern pieces.

4. Put the panels together in sets. (See step 5 below for actual sewing instructions.) Sew each red panel to a purple one, then add a black panel to each purple one. We'll end up with 6 matching 3-color sets. This is very important to keep things straight and on-grain.

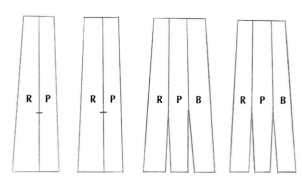

Starting 12 inches up from the bottom of the skirt, sew first a red and purple panel together, then a black one to the purple as well, to make each set.

5. Sew with a ¹/₄-inch seam allowance (this is also a great serger project). Assembling the panels a set at a time as described in step 4 above, leave the bottom 12 inches between the two panels free. Beginning 12 inches up from the bottom, backstitch to secure the seam, then sew up to the waist. The bottom 12 inches that you leave free and unsewn will create the car-wash fringes, so you want to keep them as even as possible.

6. Finish the skirt by adding an elastic waistband. My favorite method is to cut a piece of 1¹/₄-inch elastic long enough to fit my waist snugly. Stitch the elastic into a circle. Divide the elastic circle and the skirt top into quarters, and mark where the equal divisions fall on each. Then, matching the quarter marks on skirt and elastic, serge the elastic to the top edge of the skirt

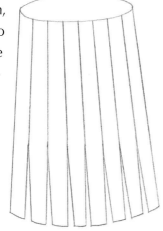

Once you have each set sewn together, sew them all to each other to make the circular skirt.

(stretch the elastic as needed to keep the quarter marks lining up as you sew). Then, turn the elastic down towards the inside of the skirt, and straight stitch along the serged edge, again stretching the elastic as needed. This makes a very simple waistband look that will never roll or twist.

elastic inside

The finished skirt with an elastic waistband has a very simple look at the top.

> **TIP**
>
> Always step into this skirt. It is not possible to pull it over your head. And, if you must use the ladies' room, this skirt will invariably end up tucked into your pantyhose. Count on it. I'm not kidding. Always do that final "fanny check" before you go back out in public.

Fashioning a Perfect Fit

Please believe me when I tell you that I am not qualified to draft a pattern. And the things I'm telling you often fly in the face of accepted industry tactics. I never pretend to be a sewing expert. I'm just a fat girl who, after years of trial and error, finally figured out how to make adjustments that worked on my body, that were easy to understand. The whole point of this book is to share that information.

Necklines and Shoulders

The Secret Adjustment That Fits

Back in chapter 7, I outlined two of the worst fitting problems we gifted women must deal with: Dinner-Plate Neckline and Dropped Shoulder Seams.

So what is the secret pattern adjustment we can make that will cure these ills? What could this magic bullet be? (Isn't this exciting?) Remember, we carry our weight below our armpits. So…just make the adjustment there!

Phyllis Krogman is a gifted friend (in more ways than one!) who worked and sewed for me and who finally got this concept through my thick skull. When she did—when I finally understood that I need to make the adjustment below my armpits—it was one of the biggest "DUH!" moments of my life!

Leave the pattern as is on the center seam. Leave the neck opening the same. Just add the extra room in the side seam—under the arm.

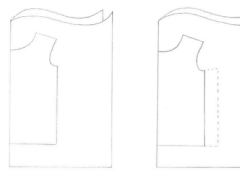

The place to add extra room in a pattern is below the armpits, where we carry our extra weight!

Obviously, making this adjustment in the side seam under the arm will make the arm opening bigger (a good thing), so we also need to add room in the sleeve pattern to make the two of them match up. It's important not to change the wrist size, however (then you would end up with a variation on the neckline problem: exploded wrists). I had a woman say to me one day, "Clothing manufacturers don't understand that our bones don't get fat." I hate to see a shirt or top that has big wide gaping sleeve openings.

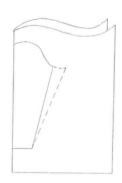

After you've adjusted the side seam under the arm, you need to make sure you adjust the sleeve pattern to match it as well. But don't add room in the wrist!

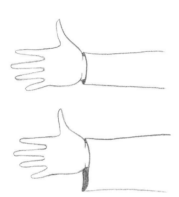

When a girl can have a sleeve that fits, why settle for a huge old floppy wrist opening?

Pants

OK, OK, you want to sew some pants for yourself. You can do this.

The pattern is the most important thing. Once you get the pattern to fit your body, you will use that same pattern over and over again. It's your choice of fabrics that will make the difference.

For your first attempt, choose a very simple pattern, one without pleats, zippers, separate waistband, etc. Look for a very basic pant pattern. Once you have selected a pattern, you do these three things:

1 First, walk into your bedroom, lock the door, take a deep breath, and take your hip measurement according to the directions on the pattern. Read the back of the pattern envelope to find out what size the pattern recommends for your hip measurement. This first step is the hardest, and it will only take about ten minutes.

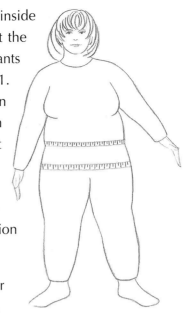

2. Now take a pair of pants that fit you and turn them inside out. Carefully drop one leg inside the other so that the pants lie flat. Now you can lay them right on top of the pants pattern piece in the size you have determined in step 1. Taking into consideration the seam allowance, the pattern piece should be slightly bigger than your old pants laid on top of them. If it isn't, you need a different size! (You might need to measure your hips again, or try different pattern sizes till you find one that matches the pants that fit you.) This comparison step is a no-brainer, but it will take another ten minutes, max, and it can save you hours of aggravation and disappointment.

3. Finally, once you found and double-checked your size, make a prototype pair of pants out of cheap, ugly fabric. Do not expect them to fit. (If you do get lucky on this first attempt, run out and buy a lottery ticket.) Keep them simple. Forget about pockets, for example. Just sew the two fronts and backs together and do a simple elastic waistband. Then try them on to see what adjustments are necessary. (Cutting and sewing this sample pair should take about thirty minutes.)

The first and hardest step is to measure your hips, which involves starting at your waist and measuring down from there. Follow the instructions on your pants pattern envelope.

Well, if you managed to do these three simple things in about an hour, you are about halfway down the road to success with pants. The rest of the journey is in making the correct adjustments, which involves some common sense (a very underrated commodity). For example, if you are a Winona, with no butt and skinny legs, you should try the prototype pants on backwards. Amazing! If you carry most of your weight in your midriff and tummy, this simple step could be the answer for you. It takes the fullness of the back seam and puts it in the front, where you need it.

As for me, I knew exactly where I needed the adjustment. To say I have a tummy problem is the understatement of the year. The awful truth is: I look pregnant all the time. That's when it occurred to me: the maternity seam! This magic seam is so simple, I can't believe I didn't think of it sooner. No fitting book I ever read told me about this. This seam accommodates a protruding stomach without sacrificing fit in the crotch, hip, or leg areas. It can be the answer for many women, and it certainly worked for me.

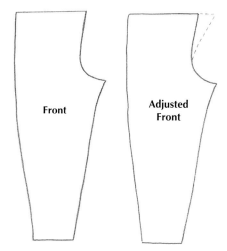

The secret maternity seam can make a pair of pants fit you all over.

As you try on your cheap prototype pants, you'll discover what specific adjustments you, personally, will need to make to get your pants to fit perfectly. But if this seems too hard to do alone, another great resource to consider is Margaret Islander's *Pants, Etc.* This is a video and workbook written and developed to help you draft your own personal pattern. You begin with just a tape measure and pattern tissue. (Note: They make longer tape measures nowadays. Get one.) Margaret does a great job with step-by-step instructions for drafting a pants pattern. This could be your answer. Ask your local sewing store if they stock this video or can order it.

Remember, once you have made all the adjustments you need and gotten a pants pattern to fit you perfectly, it will be more valuable than any algebra formula you ever figured out. So treasure it! Make sure you cut a final master pattern out of pattern trace material and mark it "final pattern." Throw out all the working copies. The sooner you lose them the better. They'll just confuse you weeks or months down the road. Put your final pants pattern in a watertight envelope or plastic bag and always keep it in the same safe place. To lose it now would be a shame. You will make it over and over again. Good luck! ▪

Index

Index